HEARTSTRINGS
FROM HEAVEN

Heartstrings from Heaven

Book Two in the Angel Bumps Series

Edited by

ANNE BARDSLEY

LUMINARE PRESS
WWW.LUMINAREPRESS.COM

Heartstrings from Heaven: Book Two in the Angel Bumps Series
Copyright © 2022 by Anne Bardsley

Printed in the United States of America

Luminare Press
442 Charnelton St.
Eugene, OR 97401
www.luminarepress.com

LCCN: 2022916836
ISBN: 979-8-88679-069-6

I dedicate this book to my dad, Jimmy Lawless.
Our home on Willow Avenue in Wayne, Pennsylvania,
was always filled with laughter.
He taught me that simple joys in life are the best.

His Irish cap keeps showing up in our house in
St. Petersburg, Florida. I think we have a visitor.

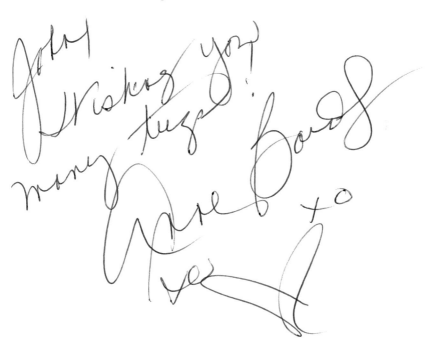

Contents

The Angel Bumps Inspiration

ANNE BARDSLEY

My mom, Bette Lawless, was the sweetest, funniest, and most loving woman. A stranger was just a friend she hadn't met yet. When my mom passed away, I felt like an orphan. I was a ship without a rudder.

The week after she died, I was driving to work in tears. "Mom, I need to know I can always find you." I continued to cry. I felt a soft hand on my cheek. "Mom, is that you? I need a sign I can't miss. I might be imagining your hand on my cheek."

I turned the corner and drove about thirty yards when my car was suddenly surrounded by little white butterflies. It was a blizzard of white butterflies. I could hear my mom laugh and ask, "Did you get that one, Anne?"

Believe beyond what your eyes can see.
Listen in the stillness for a whisper.
Trust what you feel in your heart.
For that is where Angel Bumps reside.
Love never dies.

Heartstrings from Heaven

I'm excited to bring you the second volume of stories from people across the world. The authors were carefully chosen. Each one is delighted to share their experiences.

What exactly is an "Angel Bump"?

My husband and I volunteered at the Bay Pines VA Hospital on the Hospice floor. When I'd meet families in tears, I'd tell them that their loved ones would always be close in spirit. When I shared my mom's Butterfly Blizzard sign, they would cry, hug me, and be covered with goosebumps. Most importantly, they felt comforted. I explained that those weren't goosebumps though, they were Angel Bumps. That is the feeling you get when someone you love visits you.

I feel very honored and blessed that the authors of this volume have shared stories so close to their hearts. I know how emotional it can be to write memories of someone you love. They also know the absolute joy of receiving a sign from a loved one. These stories were shared with the hope of helping others heal.

Signs can be HUGE or itsy-bitsy. Sometimes it's the smallest ones that will get your attention. If you have a feeling, pay attention to it. Don't dismiss it. If you find yourself asking, "Is that you?" chances are that you are in the presence of an Angel Bump. Someone is pulling on your heartstrings.

Some common signs are feathers, coins, dreams, cardinals, and eagles. A special fragrance, flowers, and butterflies can also be signs. My favorite is a song on the radio just when you're thinking of someone. A series of significant numbers to you may also be a sign, as well as a warm feeling, a gentle touch, something a stranger says that catches your attention, and so many more. Many of these signs were in the first *Angel Bumps, Hello from Heaven* book.

Additionally, children often deliver messages. Their innocent minds are so pure. They are very open to the spirit world. Please listen when they tell you something they've experienced.

I hope you'll find many signs in this book that resonate with you. I want the stories to comfort you and open your eyes to the spiritual possibilities in your life.

I wish you an abundance of Angel Bumps! I pray you'll feel someone in Heaven tugging on your heartstrings.

Love,

Anne

A Hallmark
from an Angel

RONNA MARTINO

When my dad passed away, I was heartbroken. Previously, a day wouldn't go by where we didn't speak on the phone. After he passed, I just wanted to call and tell him so many things. I cried the entire day of his first anniversary. My son Daniel sent me a text checking on me. I replied, "It's difficult."

He immediately texted back, "Happy Thoughts and Good Vibes."

A year later, Daniel died on my dad's birthday. I thought I'd never recover. I like to imagine Daniel surprising my dad when he walked through the pearly gates. He'd yell, "Poppy, I'm home!" A long bear hug would ensue. That vision makes me smile every time I think of Dad and Daniel.

Now I choose to live my life in Daniel's honor. I know he wants me to live a joy-filled life. Moreover, I think he has helped me along on this journey too. I certainly couldn't have done it alone.

A few months after Daniel passed, I was at Walgreens. When I checked out, the cashier said, "Wait!" and handed me a card from behind the counter. I thought maybe it was some kind of special offer. No one in front of me had received a card though.

When I got in my car, I curiously opened the card. It was a Hallmark (when you care enough to send the very best). The front of the card read, "Happy Thoughts and Good Vibes." They were Daniel's exact words to me on my dad's first anniversary! Inside it read, "All for YOU."

It was unsigned, but I knew in my heart who had sent me this card.

RONNA MARTINO lives in Duck Key, Florida. She enjoys time with her family, especially her grandchildren, and boating.

Anne Bardsley

Betsy's Bugs and Butterflies

JEANIE FOWLER

My younger sister, Betsy, was always terrified of bugs. Their hairy little bodies and long skinny legs creeped her out. If she came across one in our house growing up, she'd put a glass over it to contain it, then run out of the room. Our dad oversaw bug patrol when he got home from work.

When she married Alden, he happily stepped up as bug patrol for his new bride. He continued for the next thirty-four years.

The evening of the day Betsy passed, I needed to talk to Alden. I knew he was heartbroken and devastated. There were so many plans to attend to.

Later that evening I got a call, but not from Alden's phone. The call was from Betsy! I answered it as my heart skipped a beat. But it was Alden. His phone battery had died.

We talked and cried together as he walked through their empty house. Suddenly, he screamed, "There's a bug by the door." We both laughed and cried, remembering Betsy's phone calls to him at work and of her placing a glass over spiders, crickets, and wasps. She would even leave Post-it notes identifying the bugs! He smiled remembering his bug patrol days.

He thought that might be a comical sign from his wife, but Betsy had a better sign in mind.

Betsy loved butterflies. At her funeral, the casket was adorned with several delicately winged creatures. She looked like she was sleeping peacefully. Alden's heart was broken. He could barely hold a conversation. He loved her so much.

Last weekend, I was driving when Alden called. I put him on the car's speaker. I was always anxious to hear how he was doing. I was just ready to say goodbye when Alden said, "Wait! I must tell you why I called. You know I go to the cemetery every day to see Betsy. Yesterday, I took some butterfly decorations. It was a beautiful day with a very light breeze. All the butterflies flitted in perfect formation. When the breeze stopped, they stopped, all but one. This one continued to flutter. She was flapping her wings at me. I couldn't believe my eyes! I think Betsy was telling me she's in a good place."

Signs continued to arrive. Last week, Alden was thinking about his wife as he was driving. When he stopped, there was a car in front of him with a license plate that read: MYBETSY.

I've always referred to my sister as "My B." When she married Alden, he called her, "My Betsy." We were both very possessive of her it seems. Every time a sign arrives, our hearts get a little lighter. I love you, Betsy.

JEANIE FOWLER lives in St. Petersburg, Florida. She loves our veterans. She's escorted vets on the Honor Flight. She has three adult children and three grandchildren. She's a beach and sunshine gal.

Anne Bardsley

Triplets

ANNE MACRI

Life was going along beautifully. I was living in North Carolina with my husband and our adorable three-year-old son, Nicholas, whom we had adopted at birth, and I was pregnant with triplets after trying for years to get pregnant. With each passing day of my pregnancy, I was bonding with each of the three precious lives growing within me.

I knew where each of the three babies was situated within my growing belly. I always knew which baby was moving, I hoped and planned for the day they would come home from the hospital, and I felt so incredibly blessed to be expanding our family by two sons and a daughter.

Unfortunately, my precious babies were born prematurely after some complications. Sean and Stephen passed away while I was still delivering Christina. Christina came out crying loudly and trying to fight, and she was whisked away to the NICU. The following morning, I was told by her neonatologist that, given her medical situation, she would not survive. I held her, rocked her, kissed her, and sang to her as she passed away peacefully in my arms.

My world was shattered. I felt completely empty and broken, physically and mentally. Thankfully, our son

Nicholas was with us because he gave me a reason to get up every day.

We decided to bury our babies together in a single casket (because they were together in the womb) in a Catholic cemetery on Long Island, New York: the Cemetery of the Holy Rood. This made sense because all my family lives on Long Island and we visit them regularly, and because there was not a Catholic cemetery near us in North Carolina and we also were not convinced we would live in North Carolina forever. Holy Rood Cemetery had a beautiful area just for babies as well.

We buried our children in November, and on the first Mother's Day without them, I had a strong desire to visit them at their grave site. The first day we arrived in New York and visited their grave site, it was a typical experience, just as one might expect. I prayed, kneeled on their grave, talked to them, left little toys for them, and cried. Just a typical experience.

I wanted to return for another visit to the cemetery the next day. My husband was driving, I was in the passenger seat, and Nicholas was in his car seat in the back. While we were waiting to turn left into the cemetery gates, I had a vision in my mind's eye of my children.

The babies were not pound-and-a-half preemie infants anymore but looked to be two or three years old, and they looked so healthy and joyful! There were flowers all around them, and they seemed to be almost dancing. I remember hearing, "They came back to see us again!" This lasted only a few seconds, and in all the times we have visited since then, it has never happened again.

However, I believe this was grace that God gave me to know, without a shadow of a doubt.

Our children are together. Our children are happy. Our children know and recognize us as their family. Our children can see us and know when we are visiting them.

Our children love us. What a gift.

ANNE MACRI lives in Seminole, Florida, with her loving husband, Chris, her sons, Nicholas and Brandon, their two small dogs, and two small birds. Anne works as an occupational therapist at a local hospital.

Bells, Angels, and Ice Cream

Joanne Salemink

Time slowly robbed Mom of her mobility and memory but not her friendly smile or the mischievous glint in her eyes. After moving to the nursing home, she would sit in the doorway to her room, watching the comings and goings and giving everyone—well, almost everyone—a kind smile. That smile would still light her face every time I took her for a ride in the car, whether it was to an appointment or just to get ice cream.

And while the opportunities for mischief were fewer and farther between—no more balancing the empty chip bowl on her head to signal the waitress at the Mexican restaurant for a refill—she still made the most of little jokes. An April Fools' Day never passed without her catching someone off guard with a report of snow or mud on their scrubs ("April Fools!").

These were the stories that family and friends shared during her visitation and the funeral luncheon. Stories that made it feel like she was still with us. The stories that kept me going. But sitting graveside on that hot July afternoon, there was no escaping the fact that she was gone. Her smile, that glint in her eye—these were only memories now.

Anne Bardsley

I struggled to pay attention to the minister as he said the final prayers. The harder I tried to focus, the more my mind wandered. I was distracted by my grief, the heat, the bells. The bells?

Around me, the hush intensified. There was no sniffling. No squirming bodies or creaking of folding chairs. Even the minister hesitated.

Not bells—a recording of bells.

There were scattered quiet coughs and clearing of throats as people tried to hold back or cover their giggles. The minister powered through, trying to regain and keep our attention as the tune became more recognizable: "Turkey in the Straw."

I bent my head deeper in prayer and squeezed my eyes shut, struggling to concentrate, and trying to resist the urge to look for the ice cream truck I knew must be winding its way through the adjacent neighborhood.

Mom's and Dad's graves are only about a football field's length away from the edge of the cemetery and almost directly uphill from a "T" intersection. The ice cream truck's music was getting louder. Soon the truck would be at the stop sign at the base of the hill.

The prayer ended with a hasty "amen" and answering "amen."

And then…silence. The driver noticed our little gathering under the blue funeral home awning at last and had turned off the music. We all watched as the white truck— quietly and quickly—drove away.

And then we laughed.

"You know, Dorothy would have been the first in line at the ice cream truck," a friend said. And she was right.

Perhaps the only thing Mom loved more than ice cream was a good laugh. At that moment it felt like she was there with us, a broad smile on her face, that ornery glint in her eye. She would have wanted to see us smiling, not crying. I wouldn't be surprised if she somehow had a hand in planning that ice cream truck's route.

Whenever I remember that day (or whenever I hear the ice cream truck making its way through my neighborhood and I dash out the front door), I think of my favorite line from *It's a Wonderful Life*...or at least, my version of it:

Every time a bell rings, an angel gets ice cream.

JOANNE SALEMINK lives and writes in Eastern Iowa with her husband and their two children. She never passes up a chance to get ice cream, especially if it's from an ice cream truck!

Circus Peanuts

KIM REYNOLDS

I had the world's greatest dad. He was handsome, funny, smart, and the hardest working person I knew. Never once growing up did I hear him raise his voice or use profanity, even with five kids in the house. He was a Southern gentleman who loved us fiercely.

He had only one flaw: he believed that candy circus peanuts were the perfect road trip snack. Their shape was the only peanut thing about them. They were just a blob of waxy candy with some orange food coloring.

Every car trip as a family started the same way. First was a stop at the bank for cash, then off to the car wash to get the car shined up for the highway, and finally to the Circle-K gas station to fill up on gas and snacks. Everyone got 44 oz of their Polar Pop drink for 79 cents and their choice of snacks.

As we cruised down the road, he would dig in the brown bag, pull out his orange circus peanuts, and offer them to everyone like it was the best surprise ever.

"Dad, those are the most disgusting snack ever made. No one but you even eats those," I would say.

"What? These are great. You don't know what you're

missing. These are nice and fresh, so somebody must be buying them." It was the same on every single trip.

I would give anything to take another trip with my dad, but sadly in 2008, he succumbed to melanoma thirteen days after his diagnosis. To say I was devastated would be an understatement. I could barely function. I had lost not only my dad, but also my absolute best friend. Attempting to get back to normalcy for my children's sake, I volunteered to help with costumes for my daughter's high school play. I had to try to stay busy, when all I wanted to do was crawl in bed and sob.

One afternoon while I was sorting through the fabric in the costume room, my brother called and told me he'd had the most amazing dream the night before about dad. He said it was so real that he felt like he had spent the afternoon with him.

In this dream, my dad told my brother that he could travel. All he had to do was drop something and when someone picked it up, that would be the person he could travel alongside. The joy in my brother's voice made me so jealous. Tears began to flow down my cheeks. I wanted a sign from my dad, a visit in a dream, anything that would make me feel what my brother was feeling.

As I began to sob, I headed to the restrooms. I had cried enough over the last few months in front of strangers at the grocery store, in parking lots, and once even in the movie theater during a comedy. I needed to retreat and pull myself together.

When I exited the restroom, I decided to take the long way back to the costume room to give myself some extra time to blow my nose and apply some powder. After all this time, I knew grief couldn't be hidden, but I had to at least try.

Anne Bardsley

As I walked around the corner something on the floor caught my eye. There in the middle of the dark, abandoned hallway was a circus peanut. I thought I had finally gone off the deep end and was almost looking forward to being committed. But sure enough, when I reached down to pick it up, there was a bite taken out of it and it was as fresh and soft as my dad had often described them.

I tracked down the janitor to see if he had cleaned that hallway today, and he said he had swept and mopped it just a few minutes ago.

"You didn't see a circus peanut on the floor, did you?" I asked.

"You mean those orange candy things? No, I don't even think they make them anymore," he said.

Now I don't know if there was an old man in a teenager's body munching on circus peanuts that day, but I knew no matter how it got there, it was my sign.

To this day that peanut sits in my jewelry box along with my other valuables. It will always symbolize the wonderful times I spent traveling with my dad and remind me of the day I needed comfort and how my dad found a way to be there for me, just like he always did.

KIM REYNOLDS is sparkling her way through midlife! She is a Certified Dementia Practitioner Trainer/Senior Living Consultant whose goal is to educate the masses on senior care. When she's not saving seniors, she is a humorist and was the 2022 "Erma's Got Talent" comedy competition winner.

Freddie the Dragonfly

ANGIE BEAVER

Sadly, I lost my mum to stomach cancer in March of 2005 in England. I was in the US when I heard the news. She was seventy-six years young and otherwise in great health. She chose to pass in a hospice care facility with my dad by her side. I flew home toward the end and luckily had a full week with her before she passed. The hospice care facility had a small chapel that was nondenominational, with a beautiful, huge stained-glass window. The message from the window was not one of religion but one of dragonflies. This fable passed through generations. It's a heavenly story with a fictitious dragonfly named Freddie.

As in real life, dragonflies are born underwater, and Freddie lived with his family beneath the surface in the depths of the water. Every once in a while, one of the dragonfly's friends or family would climb up the stem of the reeds and break through the surface of the water and never be seen again. Nobody knew why they didn't come back. Freddie made a promise to his family that if he ever felt the desire to climb up the reed to where the light was bright and break through the surface, he would come straight back down to tell everyone what was up there.

One day, this pull attracted Freddie to the light, and he started to climb the reed stem. When he pierced through the surface of the water, he found himself in the most beautiful, colorful, serene place that he had ever seen. He also found that he now had developed wings and was able to spread them wide and fly.

He couldn't have felt any happier. But he remembered his promise to his family and knew that he had to go back down and share with them this incredible place. As he tried to return back through the water, he couldn't seem to get through. As hard as he tried, he just couldn't get back down to share the news of this place.

A few weeks after my mum's passing, I was working out in my garage back in Florida. I have a weight room set up there and I had the door open. Suddenly, an enormous dragonfly flew in and landed on the top of the fluorescent light. Normally, a fly like that would be zapped by the light, but this one just sat there literally staring down at me.

For a moment I was bewildered, but then I decided that it must be either my mum or a messenger from my mum. I spent my hour working out also chatting with my mum, and when I had finished, the dragonfly simply took flight and flew back out the garage door. Then, I broke down in tears, partially with sadness but more with comfort and relief.

There have often been times when swarms of dragon-flies take to the sky on our street, but they always seem to congregate by the hundreds around my car in the driveway. So now, every time I experience an encounter with one, I always feel that my mum is there with me, checking on me and my family, and I always let her know that we are okay.

ANGIE BEAVER is from Brighton, England. She has lived in Florida for thirty-three years. She's a personal trainer and fitness coach. She's been married to Steve for twenty-seven years and has three beautiful daughters.

Grandma Calling

JEANIE BROSIUS KING

I t was a sunny spring Saturday morning in Dallas when something extraordinary happened. Our precocious three-year-old son, Michael, was happily playing with his Transformer cars on the dining room floor. His dad was at work, and I was cleaning the house.

He was completely absorbed in the drama of making the cars crash and then regroup. As an only child who was around adults much of the time, Michael was an early walker and talker. Life was a constant blur of fun, mud pies, discoveries, and new ideas. He woke up chattering and went to bed with a smile on his little face.

That morning, our sleek princess-type phone perched on a low shelf suddenly rang. Michael bounced up to answer it, despite my protest: "Let Mommy get it, honey." Wiping my hands on a dust cloth, I tried to get him to give me the receiver. Ignoring me, he happily said hello and launched into a joyous conversation.

"Give Mommy the phone, please. Who are you talking to?"

He was absorbed in conversation, answering questions and laughing, when suddenly he said, "Okay. Thank you. I love you too! Bye-bye!" and hung up the phone with a huge smile and sparkling eyes.

A little exasperated, I asked him who had called. It was not normal for someone to call for a three-year-old. He grinned, nodded, and said, "It was Grandma Jean."

What? "Oh no, sweetie, it couldn't be Grandma Jean. She's in heaven with Jesus, and you never even met her. You remember seeing pictures of her, but she went to heaven before you were born."

My mother had died seven months before Michael was born, and although his little cousins remembered their Grandma Jean, Michael had only ever heard her name and seen some pictures. Really, what could a three-year-old know about his deceased grandmother?

One of the saddest parts of my life was when both my parents died at very young ages. When I became pregnant within three months of being newly married, I should have been excitedly joyful. But I felt alone and unprepared, especially with no mother to advise and celebrate my son's birth. Little questions about the care and feeding of an infant went unanswered. And this was before the days of Google or YouTube. My husband's mother was kind, but really it just wasn't the same.

Every day for years a question would pop into my head or a thought I would've liked to share with Mother, only to remember that she was gone. I sometimes wondered what she would think about this sunny and outgoing little boy who shared her red hair. Sighing, I had concluded that I would never really know.

But that spring morning changed everything.

Crouching to his level, I gathered him in a hug and said, "Honey, you can tell me who called. I need to know who you were talking to. And it wasn't your Grandma Jean. Now, who called?"

Michael stamped his little foot, put fists on his hips, and insisted, "It was Grandma Jean! That's who called me." Sitting beside him on the floor, I decided to play along. "Okay, so it was Grandma Jean calling you on the phone. What did she have to say?"

"Oh, she asked me how I was doing. And she said she wanted me to know that she is watching over me all the time. And that she sees me and loves me. And she said that she knows all about me." He grinned and jumped up. "And, she said to tell you that she is watching over you too, and she loves you!"

Done, he grabbed his cars and ran out to the backyard. Stunned, I sat quietly on the floor, rocking back and forth, tears streaming down my face. Could it be? Could my mother have reached through time and space to let her little grandson and, through him, his mother know that she is sending love and still watching over us both?

In a word, yes. There was no way a three-year-old could answer a sudden phone call and make up something like that. I now have a picture of my mother hanging near my desk, and seeing her beautiful smile and sparkling eyes, I breathe a prayer of gratitude. She might be gone, but quite obviously, she didn't leave us on our own.

JEANIE BROSIUS KING is a speaker, author, and co-founder of B-NOW Women's Retreats. You can find out more at http://beautifulnetworkofwomen.com.

Heavenly Approval

LIZ SKELTON

Growing up in a Southern family, I was blessed to spend my childhood surrounded by generations of incredible people. I knew my grandparents, great-grandmother, and even my great-great-grandmother. We spent holidays and summers in rural Tennessee on our family farm, surrounded by aunts, uncles, and grandparents.

I was fourteen when I lost my papaw. On New Year's Eve of 2008, Papaw died in a hospital bed, thirteen days after being diagnosed with melanoma. His death shattered our family, and none of us would ever fully heal. Papaw was simply one of the best men in the world. His booming laugh warmed the room, and even if you were somewhere else in the house, you couldn't help but grin when his laugh found its way to you. He was caring, giving, and had the greatest heart. He was always willing to help others.

My grandmother was the matriarch of our family. Her home was the gathering place for four generations. Despite not finishing school, she was clever, intelligent, and quick-witted. Her quips have become part of our family lore, and we still reminisce about them as if they happened yesterday. She was always certain that the women who dated her son were after him for his money and that they weren't nearly good enough for him. We always found this amusing because my uncle was not a wealthy man, unless you measured wealth by stories of less-than-great decisions. One afternoon as we discussed his latest lady, she pursed her slim lips and defiantly declared, "I'll bet she's pregnant as a goose right now." Now I'm not familiar with whether geese are overly fertile creatures, but none of us were about to question her.

Another famously quoted moment happened a few years before her death when I was a senior in high school. My mom and I made the pilgrimage to rural Tennessee to visit the family, and one afternoon we met my grandmother for lunch. We showed her photos of my prom dress. As we parted and exchanged warm, tight hugs she leaned in and whispered a solid piece of life advice into my eighteen-year-old ear: "Now, you go to the prom a good girl, and you come home a good girl." For those of you who don't speak Southern grandmother, she was telling me not to give away my virginity in exchange for a corsage.

My grandmother passed away in 2016 after a long, happy life. When she passed, part of our lives ended. We would never gather around her large kitchen table again. I was twenty-three when she passed away, and while I had begun to understand the importance of family and cherishing my time with them, I still felt like I hadn't had enough time with her.

I was blessed to be able to say goodbye to my grandmother before she passed. I arrived at her small farmhouse a few hours before we lost her. It was bittersweet to walk into the place that had served as the backdrop to so much of my childhood and see it full of family but in such a somber way. My grandmother would have been horrified that we were all fussing over her.

In the last few hours of her life, I sat in her room, held her hand, and gave her the only thing I could think to share. She'd always talked about how proud she was of me being a performer and had said she'd love to hear me sing. I'd always been too shy to sing for my family, but that day, in the small back bedroom she had slept in for more than seventy years, I sang her every hymn and church song I could think of.

A few years after my grandmother passed, I met a cute boy named Dave. On our first date, I knew he was special. Before long, I realized I loved him and that we would get married one day. His laugh reminded me of my papaw. The way he found so much joy in the littlest things in life reminded me of the smile my papaw would get on his face from the simplest things, like his gaudy cowboy piggy bank. My papa would have loved this guy, and my grandmother would have been tickled pink over his well-mannered demeanor and sweet smile.

A year later, Dave proposed. I accepted gleefully, and we planned a wedding for the following winter. The closer our wedding day got, the more I wished my papaw and grandmother were still alive. There were so many events I wished they could have seen. I wished I could have sat at the dark wooden table in my grandmother's kitchen and showed her photos of my wedding dress. I wished I could have told her about the stunning Tiffany stained glass window in the church. More than anything, I wished they could have met my future husband. I planned to walk down the aisle with one of her handkerchiefs, but I would have given anything to have her there.

My papaw would have kindly interrogated Dave and made sure he knew that he needed to take good care of his first granddaughter. Before long, they would have both been letting out deep belly laughs over their shenanigans. I knew my papaw and grandmother would have loved Dave, and I knew he would have loved them too.

One night, a week before my wedding, I had the single most vivid dream I've ever had. I have horrible insomnia and don't sleep well, so I rarely have dreams at all, much less ones that feel as real as day.

In the dream, I walked up to a small country home, through a screen door, and out into the backyard. There, sitting at a sun-soaked picnic table, was my papaw, grandmother, and even my great-grandfather, who had passed away when I was a baby. I sat with them, feeling the warm wooden bench on my legs.

My papaw was wearing a gray shirt. The slight breeze in the air carried his cologne, something I hadn't smelled in almost twenty years. My grandmother's hair was fluffed out like fresh cotton candy, and she was wearing her glasses and a black shirt with red flowers on it. My great-grandfather sat beside them. He was squinting down his nose at me.

"Tell me about this fella of yours," my papaw said with his knowing smile.

"You haven't met him?" my great-grandfather asked. "He's a good boy."

The three of them smiled at me, nodding in agreement.

It was a simple dream. but I woke up with a feeling of peace. I knew in my heart it was real. The people I missed so dearly, and who I had spent weeks thinking about, had given their blessing. Since the moments they had left my life, they had been watching me. They had seen the way

Dave loved me, cared for me, and made me smile and laugh. They loved the "good boy" who I was getting ready to walk down the aisle to, and when we got married, I knew we would bet surrounded by family, even if some of them weren't in the pews.

LIZ SKELTON is a lifelong lover of books, writing, and dogs. Her love affair with literature started early and blossomed into dreams of being the next Meg Cabot. She is currently working on her first novel.

Jenora's Feather

KAREN SHAUGHNESSY

Eight years ago, my daughter was killed by a drunk driver. I never thought I'd recover from that pain. The signs she sends me are like little gifts of love all wrapped up with a bow. I treasure them.

Just two weeks ago, we had to bury my brother. He died from COVID-19. He was autistic and childlike and loved babies. He adored my nine-month-old granddaughter, Jenora; and she, him. Her eyes would light up when he entered the room.

Recently, we were gathered at the table eating dinner, and Jenora was in her highchair. She was eating her mashed potatoes with a spoon for the first time. One spoonful in her mouth, and the next would fall onto the tray. She'd pick it up and start all over again. We laughed at her determination.

We were all sitting to the left of her when she began a conversation with someone that was not visible to us. She was looking to her right and babbling on and on, laughing and smiling for about fifteen minutes. Her chatter was accompanied by facial expressions of pure excitement. Her eyebrows raised and lowered. Her mouth puckered. She'd lean in and reach her hand out as if to touch someone.

She had 20/20 spiritual vision. I know my brother and my daughter were making her laugh. I just knew they were there. It was so beautiful, I started crying. I had to leave the room.

Afterward, Jenora sat on my lap and gently dozed off. My boyfriend, Charlie, took a picture of us. I hadn't noticed it when I was holding her. When he showed me the photo, I couldn't believe my eyes! There was a small white feather nestled in Jenora's hair.

My heart was bursting with joy. Jenora talks to angels.

KAREN SHAUGHNESSY is the mother of five and "Mema" to five grandchildren. She is an occupational therapist working with children and adults with special needs.

Kennel Karma

ANGIE KLINK

My husband and I wanted to give our son Jack a dog for his tenth birthday. It had been two years since our hyper, lovable, leather-and-paper-chewing cocker spaniel had died at the age of sixteen. I didn't want another dog as high maintenance as she had been. I longed to choose the right dog for our family of four which included Jack's three-year-old brother, Ross. But how does one choose the "right" dog? As it ends up, angels send messages in many forms—even engraved on a smelly dog pen. In my women's Bible study, we had been talking about the importance of praying for the "trivial" things in our lives for which we need guidance. Often, we are quick to pray during the huge life-altering happenings like illness, financial problems, or losing a loved one, and we think God does not want to be bothered with "everyday" requests. However, we need to remember that God is vast. He has no limits.

So even though it seemed almost silly and selfish—after all, people were living with major catastrophes out there in the world—I prayed for the perfect dog to meld with our household.

My husband Steve and I decided to preselect a dog from the local animal shelter and then return with our son on his birthday to give him his canine surprise. Steve visited the shelter first, without me. He came home and said he had found a hound mix the shelter had named Buster. I confess that a dog named Buster didn't sound like the dog for our family, but I kept an open mind to the possibilities.

I continued to pray: *Please God, show us the right dog to bring home. Is Buster the right dog?* Then together, Steve and I visited the shelter. I walked up and down the aisles of cages. Some dogs barked; others jumped on the sides of the chain-link enclosures; vying for my attention; and some sat motionless, sad eyes fixed on me. And then I found Buster. He reminded me of a dog on the old TV show *The Beverly Hillbillies*. I wasn't too sure about Buster. *Dear God*, I prayed silently as I continued my walk past the many stalls that smelled of urine and wet fur, *help me pick the right dog for our family.*

I stopped in front of a crate shared by two medium-sized, tan and white, short-haired dogs. One was standing upright, pawing wildly at the cage. The other sat shivering in the back of the stall. The one in the back had a petite build. Her almond-shaped eyes were the same caramel color as her hair. In the middle of a white band of fur at the very top of her head was a caramel-hued spot that looked like a button. *As cute as a button*, I thought.

I read the information sheet at the side of the kennel. The two dogs were sisters, about ten months old. The shelter workers had named the dog with the spot on her head Baby. I was drawn to Baby. In my heart of hearts, I knew she was the one.

I called to Steve who was on the other side of the dingy room. "I want Baby."

"I'll be there in a second," he said.

As I waited, I glanced at the top of the cage and saw a small engraved metal tag. Each cage displayed a marker bearing a name of an animal shelter donor. The tag at the top of Baby's cage read, "Cheryl Rowan."

Instantly, I felt a gut punch. Tears welled in my eyes. I knew Cheryl.

She had been a member of my church. Together, we had chaperoned a youth mission trip. She had loved animals and had volunteered at the animal shelter. Two years earlier, Cheryl had died of cancer, leaving behind a husband and two young daughters.

As I stood there on the gritty cement floor in front of the cage bearing Cheryl's name, I knew why I felt in my depth that Baby was meant for us. Cheryl, my dog-loving angel, was sending me a message.

Steve appeared next to me, unaware of the cosmic energy I was feeling at that moment. Hiding my tears and feeling a bit woozy, I stared straight ahead at Baby as she trembled in the corner. I repeated, "I want Baby."

Jack renamed her Chloe. She rests at my feet as I write this. She rests most of the time. We learned that Chloe and her sister were brought to the shelter after they were found wandering in the countryside. On her nose, Chloe has a one-inch scar, a "war wound" from her days as a fearful stray.

After we brought her home, it took Chloe several months to learn to trust us. She would hide under the furniture and look up at us, doe-eyed and cautious. When my husband would pick up the newspaper to read it, she would cower.

Chloe is gentle, unassuming, and highly precious. She is the light *click-click* of paws on the family room floor and the jingle of collar tags wafting in the air as our home's ever-present background music. Chloe greets our sons when they arrive home from school. They lie beside her on her pillow and stroke her fur. They kiss the caramel-colored spot, the button, atop her velvety soft head.

Chloe's devoted eyes look at me as if to say, "Thank you for saving me. I will love you forever." What atrocities had she experienced when she was abandoned and roaming?

Only God—and my friend Cheryl—know.

ANGIE KLINK is the author of ten books. She writes biographies, histories, and children's books. Her new dual memoir is titled *Limber as a Rag*.

Page Five

JANIE EMAUS

One look at our book of family recipes, with its grease stains and splatters of gravy, and you know it's been used. It details everything from how to make matzo ball soup to the proper way to set the Passover table. But it's more than just a cookbook. Opening the pages releases images of the women in our family gathered in various kitchens throughout the years.

My favorite aunt, who is also one of my favorite people in the world, lives on page five—Aunt Evie's Sponge Cake. She dialed direct, dishing out not only great food but no-nonsense advice. On the first Hanukkah after she had passed away, I decided to tackle her recipe.

As I lined up the ingredients, I saw her in my memory, standing in the kitchen doorway with her ever-present purse on her arm, that teacher-gleam in her eyes. She was watching and waiting. I vowed to make a sponge cake that would taste exactly like hers.

But as I learned, nothing can ever be replicated—exactly. From the start, something seemed to be against me. First, the eggs were expired. I had checked to see if I had enough but had forgotten to look at the expiration date. Well, no biggie.

From her corner perch, my aunt shook her head. "What?" I asked. They were going to be cooked for over an hour, and well, I didn't feel like making another trek to the market. I reasoned it would be fine and began separating the whites from the yolk. Not an easy task for a non-baker.

Patience, I heard my aunt's voice coach, as I groaned and picked out yet another eggshell. That advice carried me back to a conversation we'd had years ago. It was the day after I met my husband. At the time, he was separated (much like I was trying to make those stubborn eggs do) and had claimed he was heading for divorce. Yet, he was still seeing his wife.

"Give him time and be patient," my aunt had said. "If it's meant to be, it will be. You don't want to be the other woman. You want to be *the* woman."

Of course, my aunt had been right.

With that conversation in my head, I beat the sugar with the yolks until it turned a pale yellow. All was well. I added the lemon rind and some juice. The batter was progressing nicely. But then when I added the cake meal, an odd smell wafted from the batter. I had purchased the cake meal just the day before. It had an expiration date well after the next Hanukkah. I decided my sense of smell must be off for some reason. I'd come this far. I was anxious to get the darn cake in the oven.

Hmmm. My aunt adjusted her purse.

"What?" I said out loud.

What's the rush?

Once again, I thought back to those early years with my husband. After he had finally left his wife, my aunt had convinced me to give him a little time on his own. "You don't want to be the rebound relationship." Once again, my aunt had been right.

The next step for the cake was to cut the parchment paper to fit the circular pan. A function that requires an architectural degree. Or at least a sense of shapes and sizes. Skills I do not possess. Twenty minutes later, after several attempts and much frustration, the pan was ready for the batter.

The batter looked perfect as I poured it into the pan. My heart floated with joy. I picked up the baking dish from the sides and walked toward the oven.

Then disaster struck! The pan's removable bottom hadn't been secured in place.

At that moment, I realized I had never paid any attention when my aunt had made this cake. And I would never get that chance again.

I crumbled to the ground, my tears falling into the gob of batter on my lap. Missing my aunt squeezed my heart, making it difficult to breathe. I stayed on the floor for what seemed like forever. I couldn't even look up. I was sure my aunt had left me.

And then I heard her voice. *Take your time. Do it right. Those eggs were spoiled. I couldn't let you give everyone food poisoning.* I looked up as my aunt gave me her signature smile, a bit sideways with closed lips. By the time I found my keys and headed out the door for the market, she was gone.

After our Hanukkah dinner, I waited anxiously for the verdict on my cake. No one said anything for what felt like forever.

"This is delicious," my husband spoke first. "It's almost like Aunt Evie is here."

"She is," I said.

Later that night, I pulled the cookbook from the shelf and opened it to page five, now smeared with batter. And for the future bakers in our family, I slowly added the word *Patience* to the list of ingredients.

Janie Emaus is the author of the award-winning picture book *Latkes for Santa Claus*. Her next book, *Easter Eggs and Matzo Balls*, will be released in January 2023. She is a member of the Erma Bombeck writing community. Visit Janie at http://www.janieemaus.com.

A Bouquet of Pink Roses

Lola Di Giulio De Maci

I sat on the edge of my hospital bed. Empty. Broken-hearted. Devastated. My infant daughter, only nine hours and one minute old, had left me to live on the other side of the stars. She had quietly tiptoed into my life on a warm August evening and then left as quickly as she came, seeing the light of only one morning. And even though she had lived such a short time here on Earth, she had lived a lifetime and a day in my heart. She was my third and last child. I named her Angela.

Throughout the day, friends and family members wandered in and out of my hospital room, offering words and phrases of comfort. But their words were mere whispers in my heart.

"She's an angel," my mother said, trying to console me.

My best friend said, "Now she's with God."

"She's in a better place," they all said.

I know everyone tried their best to make me feel better, but none of their well-meant words worked for me. The mother in me wouldn't accept them. I didn't want an angel. And I didn't want her in a better place. I wanted her here in my arms where she belonged.

Toward evening, my niece Andrea appeared in the doorway carrying a single pink rose. She handed it to me, and I took it, holding its soft petals in my hand until the light in my room dimmed and evening slipped into the night. I placed the rose in a white paper cup and filled the cup halfway with water. That was the last thing I saw before I fell asleep. Somehow this single pink rose gave me comfort.

Since that night forty-one years ago, pink roses have taken on a special meaning for me. They catch my eye when they appear in a magazine or greeting card, on a table in a restaurant, or behind a white picket fence. They always tug at my heartstrings, leaving me breathless for the next rose to blossom on its stage.

At Mass one Sunday, the priest gave his entire homily holding a single pink rose he had plucked at random from a bouquet of spring flowers that graced the altar. I believe that rose was just for me, a message from a tiny baby who touched my life in a big way. Later that morning, I began building a spiritual bouquet of these small pink miracles, placing them at the altar I created in my heart.

In the spring following Angela's departure, my first-born daughter, Maria, made her First Holy Communion along with her second-grade classmates. My husband, four-year-old son, Christopher, and I sat in a front pew of the church, waiting for the service to begin. But something—someone—was missing.

After the ceremony, Maria posed in front of the statue of the Blessed Mother while I focused my camera. There at the feet of Mary was a crystal vase filled with a bouquet of pink roses. I prayerfully added these unexpected surprises to my mystical bouquet. "Thank you," I whispered into the sanctuary of the church. "Thank you."

There have been times in my life when I have deliberately prayed for these signs of grace to come my way—sometimes just for the sheer joy of it and, oftentimes, for the necessary boost I needed to get me through the day. I have lived twenty-three years beyond a breast cancer diagnosis and, when it comes time for my annual followup, the same question invades my mind year after year: What if? I have to muster up all the guts I can, put one foot in front of the other, and march myself into the hospital to do what I have to do.

Needless to say, I was overwhelmed with faith and gratitude one morning when the phlebotomist used a pen with a single pink rose perched on its top to write my findings on the vial. A welcomed sign. At that moment I knew I could face anything, and I would be okay—no matter what.

I then made my way to the ultrasound room and discovered that the only picture on the wall was of three pink roses, flaunting their beauty in a gilded frame. I immediately thought of my three children—a rose for each. My thoughts flew to my last baby, who quietly tiptoed into my life on a warm summer evening, staying long enough to see the light of only one morning.

"She's an angel who lives with God in a better place," they had said.

I didn't want to hear those words at the time. But throughout the years, those well-meant words have come to resonate somewhere in my soul, echoing their truth.

As I continue to gather small pink miracles to grace the altar I have created in my heart, I embrace the many blessings that arrive in the light of every new morning. I awaken to the miracle of a brand-new day, welcoming the promises and possibilities the world has to offer me.

And I am at peace.

LOLA DI GIULIO DE MACI is a retired teacher with a Master of Arts in education and English. Her stories have appeared in *Chicken Soup for the Soul, Angel Bumps: Hello from Heaven, Divine Moments,* and *the Los Angeles Times.* She also writes newspaper columns and children's books. She lives in the San Bernardino Mountains.

Sign, Sign, Everywhere a Sign

YVONNE RANSEL

Deep breaths do help, but they will never bring him back. It had been four months, and I was looking for signs from my husband, Dick, everywhere. His ashes were on the mantel in their temporary box. A permanent blue and gold one was on order after I had pursued every catalog the funeral director could find in her stash. Notre Dame had been his shining star. He had spent two magical years there. It was only fitting that his ashes rested peacefully in his alma mater's box.

I was alone in the house for the first time, sitting in my red leather chair trying to concentrate on anything but my loss. Suddenly I heard a noise, like something falling. I searched every room, up and down, for the source. My search took me to the laundry room, at the door to the garage. It was locked, the brass lever far to the right. We never locked that door, and I did not remember doing it that night. But I must have, right?

I returned to my chair and a benign episode of *Schitt's Creek* and looked up at him on the mantel.

"Did you do that? And do you want me to continue doing it?" I knew then he wanted to keep me safe forever.

From then on, the signs would come sporadically—a shiny new penny on the bathroom floor; one of his beloved hummingbirds at the feeder; a male and female cardinal at the seed cages he had lovingly kept filled.

We used to both sit at our round kitchen table, iPads back-to-back as we checked email, Facebook, and sports scores. We enjoyed our morning view of the hummingbirds and, often, Bama, our neighbors' cat, stalking chipmunks.

During COVID-19, Dick held his bankruptcy hearings telephonically from this table, in his sweats and T-shirts. The kitchen island became his back bar, filled with paperwork. What I wouldn't give to see it full and messy again.

I still sit at my usual chair and can't bear to remove his empty one, though there are times when I briefly sit there to try and witness life as he saw it. One recent morning, I noticed a shadow of the chair on the far wall behind it, where a poster of Van Gogh's olive grove hangs along with the actual photo we took of it in Arles. The shadow of the moving leaves of our forsythia danced along the chair's back. I smiled again at this new sign.

His Jeep Cherokee is still in the driveway and needs to be cleaned out and sold. However, the battery is now dead, and it will need to be charged. Our beloved pontoon boot is still floating at our pier, waiting to be driven downriver and stored. I still can't imagine anyone else at the helm, even though my son took us out on that beautiful July Sunday after the funeral. The girls did a half-hearted scream going under the bridge. It was a silly tradition he started when the grandkids were little—honking while they screamed.

Maybe he doesn't want these reminders of him to be gone from us. Maybe he keeps filling the deck and sidewalk with leaves so I must grab his favorite blower and we can do his chore together.

I went to his office today, a milestone I never thought I would reach. I was teary-eyed but not weepy as I collected two black-and-white prints off the walls—one of James Dean, the other of Ernest Hemingway. They were two of his many heroes. Maybe he put the nail in my tire to force me to visit his friend, Denny, at his repair shop just a block from Dick's office. It was Denny who squeezed my hand so hard at the funeral.

I am now so much more aware, or perhaps more open to these little bumps before me. At the *Addams Family Musical* at our local theatre last month, I stared at the top of their fascinating and clever set, where white angel wings were superimposed. Granted, that family is weirdly supernatural, but I couldn't take my eyes away from those wispy things.

And then last weekend's *Wall Street Journal* had this headline in its "Review" section: "How the Rock Concert Changed America." He had been a rock-and-roll trivia genius and could tell you not only the artist on every 45 record but its label. And if his memory failed, he would pull down his *Encyclopedia of Rock and Roll* from our music shelf and look it up.

One day this month at art class we were watching our teacher, Julie, demonstrate a new acrylic technique, when someone randomly mentioned that Gracie Slick was eighty-two that day.

We gasped and then Julie asked, "What band was she with?"

I immediately shouted over the murmurs, "Jefferson Airplane!"

"Good job, Yvonne!" I heard. But I said, "Dick just told me that."

They all smiled at my new Angel Bump.

Yvonne Ransel is a Midwest writer of essays. She lives on the beautiful St. Joseph River in northern Indiana. She is a contributor to three anthologies—*Feisty After 45*, *Laughs Out Loud*, and *Fast Fierce Women*—and writes a monthly essay for her hometown newspaper, the *Elkhart Truth*.

The Lilac Bush

DENISE DENTON THIEL

My eleven-month-old son and I both received an Angel Bump on the night my father died. Both of my parents were funny people, although their styles were very different. Mom was quick with a quip that was usually at least a bit risqué. Dad favored puns and other wordplay. Sometimes his words were four or five syllables long, and we had to get out a dictionary and look up a couple of definitions before we got the joke. Somehow that did not make the joke any less funny, and we learned something in the process.

Dad had a beautiful baritone voice, and I still remember him singing cheerfully as he got ready for work in the morning. He also had perfect pitch and taught himself to play several musical instruments.

Ours was a traditional household for that era. Dad worked six 10-hour days per week. It was Mom's job to take care of the house and the kids. Dad's one day off per week was often spent doing household repairs and taking care of the lawn. He liked repairing things, but he hated mowing the grass. He raced through the job as quickly as possible. We five children learned very early to be careful what we left lying in the yard. In his haste to get the job down, he was apt to mow right over anything in his path. He often left a trail of broken toys and a flowerbed now sprouting nothing but broken stems—the flowers chopped cleanly off their stems.

One day he mowed right over Mom's beloved lilac bush. Mom used to check it every day in the spring, watching eagerly for it to sprout leaves and then bloom. She would cut bouquets of its lush lavendar clusters and place vases of them all over the house. The whole house smelled like a fine perfume.

When he mowed it down, Mom was furious. She fussed at him about it for days, until finally he said, "I only hope someday when I am gone that you will grieve half as much over me as you are grieving over that damn lilac bush!"

Mom eventually let go of her anger, but every few weeks she would check the spot where it had been, hoping that it might survive the assault and grow back. It never did.

Dad doted on his grandchildren. When I brought my toddler son for visits, as soon as we came in the door to my parents' house, he would struggle to be put down and then run to his grandpa calling, "Papaw! Papaw!"

When Dad was only fifty years old, he suffered a massive heart attack in his recliner at home. He was already gone before the life squad even got there. They were unable to revive him.

When my phone rang that evening to give me the horrible news, I was standing on an old wooden chair and was painting a four-by-twelve-foot mural on my dining room wall. I had always loved to draw and paint. This was my most ambitious art project to date. Dad had encouraged my drawing skills and asked me often how the mural was coming. I had been working on it for weeks. It was almost finished.

My husband answered the phone and I half-listened to his end of the conversation. I knew immediately from his tone of voice that something was very wrong.

I stopped painting, climbed off the chair, and walked slowly into the kitchen.

"What is it?" I asked my husband. He gently broke the news to me that my father was dead. In shock, I looked down at the paintbrush still in my hand. It was wet with the purple paint I had been using—when the phone rang, I had been just putting the finishing touches on a lilac bush I had decided to add at the last minute.

My eleven-month-old son had been asleep in his crib for a couple of hours in his darkened room. He was a sound sleeper and seldom woke until morning, but I heard him stirring and jabbering excitedly. When I entered the room to check on him, I flipped the light switch on and there he stood in his crib with his tiny hands tightly clutching the top rail. He was staring wide-eyed at the corner near the ceiling. His eyes sparkled in excitement, and he called out over and over, "Papaw! Papaw!" I burst into tears.

I saw nothing there, but I knew that his grandpa had come to say goodbye one more time.

And that call of his passing we got just as I was painting the flowers onto a lilac bush on my mural? That was for me, and maybe for Mom, who would now grieve far more for him than she ever did for that lilac bush and its fragrant blossoms.

DENISE DENTON THIEL is a syndicated columnist for *50PlusWire* and a blogger at *Levity & Brevity*, which can be found at https://levitybrevity.com. She was the winner of the 2022 National Society of Newspaper Columnists in the humor category.

Peace from a Blue Jay

MISTY BARON

Even death cannot separate a child from a mother's love. I have no earnest recollection of why my mother appears to me from the beyond as a blue jay. It may be as simple as birds are free and, in life, freedom was what she longed for most.

Upon my maternal grandmother's passing, my mom would recall how her mother had fondly loved the cardinals. Her favorite color had been red. She had decorated her house with cardinals and fed them at her feeders. Perhaps my mom embodies a blue jay because her favorite color was blue. Or because I own antique frosted glasses decorated with colored birds: a cardinal, a blue jay, and a bluebird. There simply was a limited number of choices. Those are the birds I would recognize.

From a young age, I had an intense fear of losing my family to great tragedy. I was the eldest child, fondly doted upon. I was eight when death first touched my life. Having no experience of death, my family shielded me from my great-grandmother's funeral. Her death occurred at Christmas time. For the years that followed, my mom would sink into a deep depression around December 23. I was committed to learning a better way to experience loss.

When my grandparents eventually passed, I was in my late twenties. It was earth-shattering, but through it was born my love for angels, which had become a symbol for my grandmother.

My concept of the Great Beyond solidified with my own near-death encounter in my mid-thirties. I now know that people never die, their spirit simply transforms. The afterlife is as close to me as the hand in front of my face, simply unseen with Earthly eyes.

When cancer showed up, my mom had been unwell for over a decade. I knew more than anything that my mother longed to be free, something she could not achieve on Earth.

The qualities of a blue jay—fiercely protective and nurturing; willing to do anything to feed their family; free of worry and fear; and quietly trusting the care of the Creator— describe my mother to a T. Maybe a blue jay was what she always wanted to be.

Shortly before her last breath, I whispered to her she could go, but that I needed a sign she would always be nearby. A song was given to me that day. It begins, "I miss the sound of your voice. I miss the rush of your skin. I ache to remember all the sweet perfect words that you said."

This song became my call to her, stuck on repeat. I developed a ritual, something I call a "grief-out": an intentional time-out to experience the emotions that felt as if they would consume me. The song would play as I showered, allowing the falling water to mask the sounds of my wailing. Many days I cried. Every day I sang. I would call on my mother's spirit to dance with me as I released the stuck emotions. I would relive memories and write them anew in my heart, healed and forgiven. In those early days, I was just learning that she never died; a mental concept that made me feel good. I anchored it by repeating it to myself while asking to feel her presence.

I was not a birdwatcher in those days. I was a city girl who constantly traveled. There was no time to take up ornithology. But that didn't stop my mom from sending me a sign that first week. As a passenger traveling through a nondescript town, my attention was drawn to a blue street sign—Blue Jay Lane. I knew it was her. I knew that was our agreed-upon sign, not from a verbal discussion but from an understanding that the blue jay would be a symbol of her unwavering presence in my life.

During the months of grief-outs, blue jay imagery showed up in fun ways, and I was primed to notice: a friend sent a T-shirt embellished with a blue jay; ball team mascots appeared at random stops along my way; and numerous other signs appeared as I asked for them. Our relationship had transcended her death. I could call on her with a simple thought, no matter where I was.

I found this to be true while working at a pristine resort in Guam with a crew of four during a pandemic lockdown. The entire island felt like it was all for me. It was the most glorious experience, one that rated a gushing call back home. The day of work had been hard, so as I showered, I played her song and asked her to show up for me. The thought crossed my mind that it would not be possible for her to signal me. The North Pacific Ocean is not a blue jay habitat. I shoved that thought aside. I told myself not to discount my desire, simply to allow and trust.

Just a few hours later as we walked a mall waiting for our food, I rounded a corner and my friend pointed out the Swarovski store window. To my utter amazement, there stood a precious sign, her sign, calling to me that she had heard me: a blue jay made of the most brilliant crystal standing over a foot tall. She was there in the most unexpected way!

It was nearly eighteen months later that my mom showed up as an actual living bird. I had stopped asking for signs for quite some time, but this day grief was there, and I was its captive. Feeling tired and worn, I escaped into the bathtub. I prayed for rejuvenation, vitality, and to have my cup filled. Cognizant of the power of a blue full moon, the energies of Día de Los Muertos, and the healing landscape surrounding me, I asked that my mother show herself that day.

She responded that evening in Canyonlands National Park, Utah, by flying past me twice as a single male blue jay! Then, a short time later at a picnic spot, she made a second appearance, this time as a momma blue jay singing her song to my face. This is what she said: "Moms never die. We are never alone in this place. Loved ones, tribe, and faithful servants are beyond our sight but never beyond our reach. We impose our limits. But if we choose, we can scale mountains simply by asking for Divine help. It is as easy as asking and believing in the receiving of the assist. Support surrounds us now."

A tear fell quietly, but this time it was a tear of joy, amazement, comfort, and peace.

MISTY BARRON is a near-death experiencer turned spiritualist after a medical mishap. She found happiness through "laughter yoga." She healed herself and now lives a life of infinite joy through travel and service with her husband.

The Tattoo Appointment

LISA MARLIN

I had made the same appointment nearly every year and canceled it whenever I decided it was a crazy thing to do at my age. But on the eleventh anniversary of Mom's passing, the same month I turned fifty-five, I went through with it. I'd lived without nipples long enough, and it was finally time to get some new ones in permanent ink.

The cancer had taken my real nipples from me. The right one, along with my whole right breast, went first in 2003 when I was diagnosed with breast cancer. I opted to get implants in both breasts to feel and appear somewhat normal. In 2010, the left implant ruptured, and I needed surgery to replace it. My doctor highly recommended removing the whole left breast, nipple included, since my mother and one of my sisters had had cancer return a few years after their first diagnoses. Though my sister survived both early-stage cancers, Mom's second diagnosis came too late for treatment to save her, and she died in 2007.

I agreed with my doctor, thinking then that it was only my last nipple, not my last hurrah. I had plenty of living left to do, and if slicing that little protrusion off my body meant I'd have a better chance to do that, then off with it!

Over the years, I'd also convinced myself that I was selfish to think it mattered at all that I didn't have them anymore. But every year near the anniversary of Mom's exit to heaven, I felt an urging to do something about it.

When I told my partner that I had decided I was going through with the appointment this year, he supported my decision and reminded me it didn't matter to him. But it did matter to me. I would be the one seeing them each time I stepped out of a shower that faced a mirror and each time I changed in the locker room at the gym. Every time I glanced down at my naked chest, I would see something resembling nipples. Instead of just deep pink scars running halfway across each bare mound where the implants had been inserted to replace life-threatening tissue, I would see small circles shaded in the color of my lips.

I wouldn't have any more physical sensation there than I'd had since the mastectomies, but I was hopeful that I would be mentally strengthened knowing that cancer had not completely erased this part of me.

As the hour of the appointment drew closer, I grew more nervous. What if this experienced nipple tattoo artist, who was also a nurse practitioner in the plastic surgeon's office, wasn't as good as her colleagues touted her to be? What if the dozen pretty photos she showed me of her previous works were the only good ones out of hundreds more dissatisfied clients?

I could almost hear my mom answer with a question of her own: But, Lisa Ann, what if they turn out beautiful and make you happy?

I arrived at the clinic surprised at how emotional I'd become. When the artist came into the room and began organizing the ink and equipment, I couldn't hold back my tears. She stopped her busyness and gently rested a hand on my shoulder as I told her about losing my mom on this exact day eleven years ago. I told her that I should've known better than to schedule it on this date. The artist nodded and took a deep breath, matching my own. She told me she was honored to be a part of this special experience and promised she'd do her very best to make sure I'd like the results.

As I lay back and the needle penetrated my numbed skin with the ink, I couldn't refrain from mentioning how silly I felt to be doing this to a part of my body that was mostly always covered up. "It's not like I plan to go showing off my new paint job to anyone," I said, right as the buzzing tattoo gun silenced.

"Well, this has never happened before," the artist said as she stood up straight and stepped back. "The lights are on, but for some reason, the electrical current got interrupted."

I watched as she adjusted the cord and manipulated the controls on the machine to no avail.

"Maybe you should ask your mom to step in so we can finish," she said as seriously as if Mom could indeed walk over to the machine and fix it.

I shrugged as I said, "Hey, Mom, can you help us out here?" Suddenly, the buzzing resumed. The artist and I looked at each other, eyes wide as we both laughed. "I think she wanted me to stop second-guessing myself. You won't hear another negative peep from me."

"Yes, please don't do that again," the artist said, smiling as she stepped back to my side, the tattoo gun ready in her hand to finish the work she'd begun.

In the months that have passed since then, I am very pleased with my new hidden features and especially happy that Mom showed up to make sure I'd quit questioning the why of it. The tattoos are beautiful, and that's all that matters to me.

Lisa Marlin is a contributor to several anthologies, newspapers, and magazines. She credits her family as her greatest source of joy, worry, and writing prompts. Lisa lives in Colorado, where she enjoys a spectacular mountain view from her front porch every single sunshiny day. You can find her at https://www.lisamarlin.com.

A Garden Stopover

SARAH DEMAREST GUTHRIE

Of all the people back home, I would have figured I'd have made it to *her* funeral. Mrs. Landiss was my neighbor, my English teacher, and the one who ironed my dress for my father's funeral. She had also picked me up at the airport more times than I can remember when Mother was sick and dying.

Before the house was sold, Mrs. Landiss helped me rescue bulbs and plants from Mother's yard to pack up and take to Kansas City. She added lily of the valley and double daylilies from her own garden. On one of my last trips, we visited Mother's wildflower garden, where she showed me the bloodroot and winter aconite. They were early spring flowers, so the blossoms were gone, but she recognized the leaves. She reminded me that bloodroot is like a small daisy; aconite is like a shimmering buttercup. We carefully dug up the plants so I could recreate a wildflower garden of my own. She had loved the bloodroots' buttercup color and especially how they shimmered in the sun.

She was never too busy to help, offer advice, or just be a friend. But when her time came, it caught me at a period when my own life was gridlocked. Too much would fall through the cracks if I dropped everything and flew home.

Instead, I sent my regrets and flowers and slogged through the deadlines of work, kids, and life. She would have understood I knew, but I was sad.

The day after the funeral, I was walking by my garden. It was March, and not much was peeking out of the mulch. Except for the aconite. We had saved it from Mother's wildflower garden years before, she told me it was one of the earliest spring flowers...and there it was.

And suddenly, so was she. It was as if she stopped by on her journey to heaven to say hello. Her warm presence was lingering in the garden. She stayed for a while, too, as we looked at the garden that held so many memories. I thanked her for coming...and then she was gone.

I thought I would never feel her presence again, but I was wrong. She comes back in the spring, as if to check on the flowers and me. And she still shimmers, just like her favorite flower, in my heart.

SARAH DEMAREST GUTHRIE grew up in an unairconditioned house in sultry Tennessee. Today, she writes to raise money for nonprofits in Kansas. In her dream world, she writes children's books and heartwarming stories.

Chandler's Message

AMY INNARELLI

My son Chandler was twenty-two when he died. It was Christmas Eve, and Chandler had plans to pick up his girlfriend and their son. They were headed to his sister's house for the night after their Christmas Eve party. He was murdered while sitting in his car waiting for them to come out of their house. Our lives were changed forever.

Since he left us, I've received so many signs from him. He wants me to know he is still close to me. In fact, I just experienced the most beautiful message and Christmas gift I could have ever asked for and had to share. It's that amazing!

While out running the last few errands before Christmas Day, I was listening to Matt Fraser's book *When Heaven Calls* on Audible.

Upon getting into my car after leaving Party City where I had picked up the balloons for our celebration, Audible immediately connected to the book again; however, it stopped abruptly. I heard Chandler's voice in the speakers. One of his voicemails played: "Just wanted to tell you, I love you." Nothing more, nothing less, that was all it played. Then my book started up again!

This has never happened before.

I sat there in disbelief for a moment and then immediately grabbed my phone. I quickly caught myself trying to explain how that could have happened and decided to simply live in and enjoy the beautiful moment, to which I replied with a tearful smile from ear to ear: "Thank you, I love you too, Naners. Merry Christmas!"

Naners is one of my nicknames for him. There was an episode on the TV show *Friends* where Chandler received mail addressed to "Chanandler Bong." We nicknamed our Chandler "Chanans." We then shortened it to "Naners."

I believe.

AMY INNARELLI is the founder of the Chandler's Angels Initiative. This organization brings awareness of healthy alternatives for communities to prevent violence.

I Am with You Always

CINDY DEROSE

God blessed me with an angel for my mom. We shared an incredibly special bond. I used to talk to my mom every day. We were best friends. And our bond is still so strong since she went to Heaven on September 16, 2021. God sends his angels to give me signs from my mom that she is at peace with Jesus, my dad, and all the other angels. I loved my mom so very much.

In May 2021, at the age of eighty-nine, my mom had a mild heart attack, a mild stroke, and a clot in her right leg. Her cardiologist said most people would not have survived that combination, but my mom had a strong will to live for me and our family. We all loved her so very much.

A few months later, my mom arrived in Heaven, from where she called my name as I was waking up from a dream. I heard "Cindy," said calmly in her tone of voice. She sounded like she wanted to tell me something.

Just two days after my mom went to Heaven, I found a white feather. I had asked God as I looked at the rising sun to send me a sign that my mom was at peace with Jesus and my dad in Heaven with all the other angels. At that exact moment, I looked down and found a white feather at my feet. I learned the meaning of finding a white feather. It means your guardian angel is watching over you, the end of pain and suffering, and a new beginning. Mom always said when you go to Heaven, it's a new beginning.

That evening I went to Ashtabula Harbor on Lake Erie with my husband, Lee, and some friends for a boat ride to watch the sunset. When we got there, I was overcome with grief and missing Mom. I just wanted to pick up the phone and call her about the beautiful evening we had planned. I told my husband, "I don't know if I can live life without Mom." Just as I was stepping onto the boat, a feather appeared on the grass. I knew it was a sign from God and Mom. The boat driver told me it was the most incredible sunset they had seen all summer.

On November 29, 2021, a heart was carved in the snow in my driveway. It didn't melt overnight like three-quarters of the driveway had. When the snow did finally melt, underneath I found a heart of crushed leaves. This was the exact spot I found the other white feather.

After my mom went to Heaven, I created a garden in memory of my parents with flowers that bloom in the spring and an angel statue with a water fountain. Just as we finished it, a tiny white butterfly flew over it as the sun shone down. It became our visiting place.

Recently, my parents became great-grandparents! Eleanor was born nine months to the day of my mom's passing. Mom would have felt so honored to have a little namesake. I wish she could have been here to meet this little sweetheart.

Not so long ago, I was looking at the sky and said, "I know you are smiling in heaven." Just then, two cardinals flew by together. They landed in the tree next to my parent's memorial garden. Then a white butterfly joined them.

My Mom is still with me in spirit and soul, loving me from Heaven. Her spirit is alive in my heart. Love is eternal.

"What we once enjoyed and deeply loved we can never lose, for all that we love deeply becomes part of us."

—Helen Keller

CINDY DEROSE lives in Ohio with her husband of thirty-three years. She enjoys photographing God's gift of nature. She is also a wellness and antiaging advocate. Contact her at cindy.derose@icloud.com.

Miraculous Medal

PAT BOSILJEVAC

I was ordering a Miraculous Medal for my niece, Trisha, a nurse at Cincinnati Children's Hospital. It was to be a surprise delivery. To get free shipping, I had to spend an additional five dollars. So I added a little biography of the Miraculous Medal. The next day, the little book shipped.

Would she wonder why she was getting the biography—of course, she would. I told her half of the shipment was coming and the other half would be there soon. When I didn't get the shipping notice a couple of days later for the actual medal, I called the Catholic Shoppe. The very nice man understood why I was anxious to have it sent. With the virus going around, we all needed extra protection.

He offered to call another jewelry store and have one sent from there. It wouldn't be the same medal, but it would be of comparable quality. A few days later, Trisha received it and was thrilled. Since receiving the medal, she hasn't taken it off.

A day or two later, I received a shipping notice for a Miraculous Medal from the Catholic Shoppe. I quickly emailed them and explained that they had already sent it, she loved it, thank you very much, end of story—not!

That was two to three weeks ago. This past Saturday, Trisha called to tell me the bad news. Her daughter Kira was heartbroken. Her older cat, Sparkle, had to be put to sleep. That cat had been a part of Kira's life since she was four, and she *loved* her. Kira was devastated. It had only been a few months since Kira's Grandma Janet had died. This was too much loss in such a short time.

Here's the Angel Bump: Saturday afternoon in their mailbox was a delivery from the Catholic Shoppe. Another beautiful Miraculous Medal on a lovely chain had arrived. Not the same one Trisha has but equally beautiful. No notes, no receipts, just the package. Kira immediately put the Miraculous Medal on and asked Trisha, "How did Grandma do that? How did she get this to me?" Trisha just smiled. Sometimes a grandma just knows what her grandchildren need.

When Kira's dad saw it, he asked where she got her Miraculous Medal. Kira just smiled and said, "Grandma sent it to me. She knew I needed it today."

He was speechless.

PAT BOSILJEVAC lives in Landrum, South Carolina. She is a wife, mom, and grandmom. She has a strong faith and loves the Blessed Mother.

Straight from Heaven, A Message from Dad

Lynne Cobb

My dad passed away a little over two years ago. I still miss him. He was my go-to guy when I felt anxious. He didn't always try to fix things; most of the time, he just listened.

The father-daughter bond we shared was very strong, and even though I can't physically see or hear him, I think of him daily, and I believe he communicates in his special way.

For instance, a few hours before my dad passed away, we experienced an early evening mid-summer storm. Fierce winds, thunder, lightning—the works. A vibrant and most beautiful rainbow appeared shortly after the storm, and for several months after his death a rainbow continued to appear monthly on the same date—the twenty-third day of each month. Anyone who has lost someone so dear often marks the monthly anniversary until it becomes a yearly observation. (Oh, this was amazing too—a rainbow appeared on the first Father's Day we celebrated without him.)

I will be going about my day, thinking of Dad, and then his favorite song, "September," will play on the radio or his favorite hymn, "Amazing Grace," will be listed in the church bulletin. During times of incredible stress, I have seen Dad in my dreams. He says nothing, but he has the most peaceful smile and always hugs me. It is all too vivid and the timing is way too perfect to be called a coincidence.

When fall rolls around, I think of him constantly. Anyone who knew my dad also knew he had an immaculate yard, and during the fall, he declared a full-on attack on the leaves. Yes, this is the man who would stop mid-conversation to go outside and grab a leaf off the front lawn. And yes, this is the same man who "slid" off the roof and broke his leaf blower because, yes, he was on the roof, ridding it of leaves, so that they would not land in the yard.

During Dad's eulogy, our pastor shared these stories with all who came to celebrate his life. There was so much laughter. Seriously, who gets on the roof and, essentially, rakes it? One year, my siblings and our spouses wanted to bring bags of leaves and dump them all over the yard as a prank, so that when Dad grabbed his morning paper, he would be greeted with three to four inches of leaves covering every blade of grass. We didn't because, well, we knew that could have caused a major health event. We didn't want to bear that burden for the rest of our lives!

When we interred Dad's ashes in a memorial garden at church, there was a hush of quiet as our immediate family gathered. It was a pretty fall day, and the earlier rain had subsided in the nick of time. The pastor was reading scripture and said a prayer. Then there was a murmur, which turned to some mild snickering... because in the spot where Dad's remains would eternally rest, in that just-opened space in the memorial wall, what does our pastor find? A leaf. He wondered if we should remove it or leave it there to drive Dad crazy for all eternity.

See what I mean? I swear he sends us messages from beyond.

Well, I have needed my dad these past few weeks. What I wouldn't give to just talk to him. I still do, I guess what I want is to hear his voice.

This past Sunday, after worship, my youngest daughter and I took a stroll through another garden at church. It was a nice walk, and we had just heard our pastor's sermon about angels. The garden, still sporting some roses in the early fall, was peaceful and pretty, with a calming fountain and lots of stones with scripture verses along the path.

Halfway through our walk, one stone stood out to me because, of all things, there was a leaf lying on it. One lone leaf, which, of course, caught my eye. Any time I see a random leaf, I can't help to think of dear old Dad.

Oh my gosh…I had to grab my phone and snap a photo, because I honestly could not believe my eyes! Straight from heaven—a message from Dad!

Right under the leaf, the scripture verse read: "'Do not be anxious about anything.' Philippians 4:6."

Teary-eyed and a little shaken, I looked up and whispered, "Thanks, Dad."

LYNNE COBB is a speaker, writer, journalist, artist, and editor of a monthly newspaper. Visit her at https://lynnecobb.com for more enjoyable stories.

The Purple Butterfly Connection

Jennifer Fleck

I was in fourth grade when my family moved into an apartment complex in Oaks, Pennsylvania. A family with a girl my age moved in above us. I didn't know how to introduce myself, so I made her two pink gimp bracelets. I learned her name was Keeley, and after a few days, we became friends. We would listen to music for hours. Keeley's favorite musicians were Kurt Cobain from Nirvana and Dave Pirner from Soul Asylum. She was very upset when Kurt Cobain died.

As time passed, we became closer. Keeley would talk about the back brace she had to wear due to her scoliosis and how she loved her Adidas Gazelles. Keeley was a tiny girl but very happy! Our days of hanging out came to an end when her mom, Nancie, moved to a new apartment. My family moved a year later as well. But Keeley and I still talked on the phone regularly and kept in touch. During our last conversation, we shared stories and said we had to make plans to get together.

A friend gave me the horrible news that Keeley had died in a car accident. My heart sunk, and I just couldn't

Anne Bardsley

believe or understand why. Why Keeley? Why could I enjoy my eighth-grade formal and Keeley pass away? We had just talked about hanging out. Why did God have to choose her?

I went to her funeral, and so many people were there. I think most of our school attended. There were so many flowers and even more tears. I remember the song "For You I Will" as the *Space Jam* soundtrack played. I couldn't imagine what her mom and the rest of her family were going through and would continue to go through for years afterward.

I couldn't go to the cemetery though; it was just too much for me. I did visit her grave when I could after, and I would break down every time. But when I moved to Philadelphia, I couldn't make it up to see her as often.

Many years later, I moved back to Oaks. One day I had errands to run, and I brought my youngest son along. Justin was six at the time. He is on the autism spectrum, and he's high functioning. After we finished, I took a long way home. I knew we were coming close to the cemetery. I went back and forth with myself about stopping, but something told me to stop. So I told Justin we were going to go see Mommy's friend. He asked her name, and I said, "Keeley." Confused as to where we were, he asked, "Why are we here?" I explained, "This is where Keeley is."

I knew I had parked close to her site, but on this day I couldn't find it. Justin was still asking questions behind me as I wandered around. Suddenly, Justin yelled, "Mom, what is her name again?" I said, "Keeley." He called me over. He was standing right at her grave. Somehow, I had walked right past it. An indescribable feeling came over me. I felt like she had led Justin right to her.

We stood there as my tears fell. After a few minutes, Justin turned around and noticed a purple plastic butterfly on the ground about two feet away. I said to him, "That must be Keeley's. She loved purple butterflies. Let's put it in the flowers that are on her grave." I was so overwhelmed with emotions. It was such a small thing, but I felt it was a connection between Keeley and Justin.

When we got back in the car, I messaged her mom to tell her what had happened. She said, "The butterfly has been missing for a month. I'm so glad Justin found it and was able to return it to its home." After talking to Nancie, I felt this calming yet heavy release. I do believe we were in the right place and time for all of this to happen. I miss Keeley so much! I know she would be the greatest Aunt Keeley if she were alive today. It seems she and Justin had already met. Until we meet again, forever rest in peace, Keeley! 11/26/1980–4/18/1997. I love you!

***

JENNIFER FLECK was born and raised in Montgomery County, Pennsylvania. She volunteered and works as an EMT. She enjoys spending quality time with her family.

Anne Bardsley

The Other Love of His Life

AMY PATUREL

My fiancé's first marriage ended in tragedy. Before we could be happy together, he had had to make peace with that. And so had I.

Before we were engaged, I woke up to his kisses on a warm morning in July and felt guilty. It was her birthday, and I was at her house. With her husband. In her bed. Her bookshelves were filled with the same books I had on mine: *The Cider House Rules*, *Beloved*, and *The Pilot's Wife*. She had been a literature professor. She had loved writing. She had loved reading. She had loved Scrabble. And now she was gone.

Brandon had been married for less than six months when his wife was killed in a car accident. When I met him two years later, he was still wearing his wedding ring but on his right hand. I assumed the ring was a symbol of his continued commitment to her. Not a sign that he was ready to build a life with someone new.

Beyond the ring, there were a million reasons why I should have passed Brandon by. I love books. He never reads. I live near the beach. He's seventy-four miles inland. I'm a health nut. He subsists on Buffalo wings and beer.

But there were bigger reasons for me to stay. We both loved racing toy penny cars in the mall, pretending we were Fred Astaire and Ginger Rogers, and singing Barry Manilow's "Copacabana" at the top of our lungs. He was loving, charming, and sweet—and he knew how to make me laugh from deep within my belly.

Plus, I was like her. And they were happy. I pored over her pictures trying to learn everything I could about the woman who came before me. She would always hold a place in Brandon's heart, so I needed to know who she was.

A chill came over me when I visited her memorial page and read through the online guest book: "No one could ever fill her shoes," someone had written. That launched me into my next search: "dating a widower." Every site I visited warned of men who disappear after a few months out of guilt; those who constantly draw comparisons to their late spouse; and those who live in the tragic state of "what if?" Brandon hadn't done any of those things. But then I read this: "If he has pictures of her on the walls, clothes of hers in the closet, and trinkets of their life together on display, he is not ready."

Brandon insisted he wanted to move on, that she was dead and he was not. He didn't trigger any of the red flags I had read about. About a month into the relationship, the ring came off. Pictures were tucked away and replaced. Slowly, her clothes began to disappear from the closet.

Yet I still grappled with the feeling that I might never measure up to what he had lost. In his mind, she will always be thirty-three and beautiful. Me? I'll get gray hair, wrinkled skin, and flabby thighs. What's more, their relationship will remain perfect, frozen forever in newlywed bliss. In their six short months together, they hadn't weathered the storms

Anne Bardsley

that come with age and time: sleepless nights caring for newborns, arguments over money, in-law drama.

As I fell more deeply in love, more questions came. If he had to pick one of us, whom would he choose? After we die, will he want to be buried next to her or me? Will we spend eternity as a trio?

But the most pressing question came on the morning of July 12: Do I go with him to visit her at the cemetery?

At first, I thought I didn't belong there, that she would want to spend her birthday with her husband minus the new girlfriend. I felt guilty for living the life she was robbed of—that I was lucky because she wasn't.

But Brandon reassured me. "She would want me to find someone else," he said. "Someone who can make me as happy as she did."

So, we celebrated her birthday together—all three of us. Brandon and I arranged flowers and planted a mini balloon in the earth. "She's usually pretty quiet," he said, trying to get a laugh. The wind kicked up and the balloon began bobbing back and forth. "It looks like she's waving at us," I said. Secretly, I hoped she was letting me know she approved.

At that moment, I realized I didn't want to fill her shoes. I had my own. She and I had much in common, but we were also very different. I call Brandon out on things she might have let slide. She enjoyed shopping; I prefer wine tasting. She was a master quilter: I can't hem a pair of pants.

"I am a very lucky man," Brandon said, as he hugged me on the cemetery lawn.

I used to disagree. How could someone who lost his wife in an instant call himself "lucky"? But as we walked back to the car, I knew he was right. He has the love of two women.

Maybe I'm a hopeless romantic, but I like to believe the first one helped guide him to the second.

---

*This story first appeared in *Newsweek*.

AMY PATUREL is a writer in Southern California whose work frequently appears in the *Los Angeles Times*, the *New York Times*, the *Washington Post, Good Housekeeping*, and many other publications. An award-winning essayist, Amy also teaches personal essay writing to students across the globe.

Scent from Heaven

GEORGIA A. HUBLEY

Growing up, I gave my dad his favorite Old Spice after-shave lotion every year for Christmas and Father's Day. Dad wore this lotion every day. I, too, have always loved that fresh, clean fragrance in the white glass bottle with the blue sailing ship insignia and the Old Spice name written in red script.

How grateful I am for Old Spice's aftershave lotion. Because last spring, I was awakened by a burning sensation in my nose, and within seconds the familiar sweet and spicy aroma of oranges, nutmeg, and vanilla soothed my nostrils. I had been sleeping soundly on my left side, but suddenly I found myself sitting upright in bed with the left side of my body numb and tingling from the neck down to the bottom of the foot.

I struggled to catch my breath, as the overwhelming presence of my dad's signature scent permeated the air in the bedroom. Sometimes a whiff of a familiar scent triggers nostalgic memories that make me smile, but this powerful scent was different and sparked a vivid emotional memory: Dad retired at sixty-seven, and two days later he had a stroke and was paralyzed on the left side. He never fully recovered.

My mind swirled with thoughts and concerns about what was happening to me. After all, I had regular check-ups. It'd been a year since I last went to the emergency room for chest pains, and after many tests, no heart issues had been found. My diagnosis had been a severe case of indigestion.

I shivered as I rushed to put on my most comfortable yoga pants, a big shirt, and flip-flops. I wondered what if I'd remained in a deep sleep? Would I have had a stroke and been paralyzed like my dad? Suddenly, a strange calm came over me, and I knew I must heed this strange aromatic warning and head to the hospital nearby—pronto!

My husband is an early riser, and I am not. I'm a night owl and write during the wee hours. My husband's daily morning routine begins with an early three-mile walk. My day begins later than his. Since our two sons are grown and the nest is empty, this schedule works for us. However, I knew if my husband hadn't returned from his early morning hike, I'd have to call 911.

"Are you home?" I shouted as I stumbled down the stairs.

As soon as my husband spotted me fully dressed and not in my robe, he realized something was amiss. "What's happened? You're never up this early."

"I feel weird. I'm numb and tingly from my neck to my toes." I grimaced.

"We're heading to the ER," he said.

We reached the hospital in six minutes, and due to my symptoms, I was seen right away. The emergency room medical personnel evaluated my condition. They determined I needed additional tests and scans, and I was admitted to the hospital. On the first day, nothing was found, but the numbness and tingling on my left side had diminished.

Then on the second day during an angiogram, two blockages were detected in my coronary arteries. During the procedure to remove the blockage on the left side of my heart, one stent was inserted to keep the artery open, and during the second procedure to remove the blockage on the right side of my heart, two stents were inserted to keep the artery open. My cardiologist was pleased with the results and my recovery.

I'm thankful for modern medicine, and it is a miracle I am alive. Indeed, that scent from heaven saved my life.

I must admit, during my teenage years, I didn't always appreciate my dad being my protector, but as an adult, I understand why he was often overly protective of me, "his little girl." I'm grateful Dad is still protecting me and is my guardian angel.

---

* This story was originally featured in *Woman's World*.

GEORGIA A. HUBLEY retired from Silicon Valley's money world after twenty years to write about her own world. Writing credits include *Guideposts*, *Woman's World*, *Chicken Soup for the Soul* series, and many more.

Grandma's Rings

STACEY GUSTAFSON

Mom filled her largest bowl with assorted bags of candy, including Milky Way, Snickers, Twix, M&Ms, and licorice. In St. Louis, Halloween tradition demands that kids tell a joke to receive a sweet. A simple "trick or treat" will not do.

Ding-dong. The doorbell signaled the start of Halloween. Time for Mom and Grandma to hold court on the front porch. The smallest kids arrived at dusk, tripping over each other to get the treats.

As the kids reached the top step, Grandma asked, "What's your joke?" She perched on a wrought iron chair, surrounded by glowing jack-o-lanterns and spooky cardboard cutout ghosts, as the kids recited carefully memorized corny jokes. From the oldest to the youngest, all ages were expected to participate.

A preteen dressed in a pirate's outfit with a white swashbuckler shirt and a red vest edged with gold brandished a wooden sword and yelled, "What's a skeleton's favorite musical instrument?"

"What?" asked Grandma, clasping her hands to her chest.

"The trombone," he said. He snatched a handful of candy

Anne Bardsley

from the bowl, stuffed it into his orange plastic pumpkin, and rushed off to join his mom at the curb.

"Why did the golfer wear two pairs of pants?" said Alice in Wonderland, dressed in a buttoned blue dress with puffed short sleeves and a white pinafore apron.

"Why?" asked Grandma, leaning in.

"In case he got a hole in one," she said with a laugh.

In her lap, Grandma gripped a cup, a tall plastic container decorated with a witch's face featuring a crooked nose and wart. A purple witch's hat was mounted on top of the mug. Squeeze the handle and the top popped open, revealing a jumble of black and orange plastic spider rings. After a kid told a joke, they moved in for a turn to open the mug.

"Hahahahaha," cackled the mug.

The tiniest of trick-or-treaters sidled up to my grandma, dressed as a mermaid with shimmering greenish-blue pants and red hair. Before Grandma could ask if she had a joke, the child put her pudgy hand on my grandma's arm.

"What's that?" the mermaid said with a soft voice and eyes that danced.

"It's a witch's cup," Grandma said. "It's filled with magic. Want to see?" Then she pressed the handle and poured out a few spider rings into the child's outstretched hand.

"Thank you," the mermaid said with a wide smile.

Grandma waved, "See you next year," as the child rushed back to her mother.

That was the last Halloween Grandma celebrated at my mother's house. She passed away the following year after a struggle with complications from cancer. Near the end, we stayed by her bedside for days.

One evening the doctor approached us. "Ladies, it's okay to leave," he reminded us. "Go home and sleep in your bed.

We'll call you if anything changes."

I kissed Grandma goodbye, and we held hands as we left the intensive care unit, unaware that this would be the last time we would see her. At home, we tried to cheer each other up with stories of Grandma.

"Remember how she enjoyed Halloween?"

"The kids loved her witch's mug."

"I'm going to miss her stories."

We fell asleep around midnight, exhausted from the vigil at the hospital. At 3:15 a.m., a shrill ring broke the silence.

Brrrrrring. Brrrrring. Brrrrring.

It stopped as abruptly as it started.

"Mom," I said, straining to hear movement from the other room. "Did you hear the phone ring?"

"Yes," she said clearing her throat. "That's weird."

Was Grandma sending us a message?

We had trouble falling back asleep but woke when the phone rang again at 7:00 a.m.

"Sorry to tell you that your mother passed away early this morning," said Grandma's ICU nurse, Shannon.

The following year, my mother continued the Halloween tradition of handing out candy. "You'll never believe what happened," Mom said to me on the phone afterward. "It was like Grandma was telling me to remember to put out the treats for the kids." "Tell me more," I said.

On the night before Halloween, Mom's boyfriend helped her set up the porch and decorate the house when a crackling sound erupted from the basement.

"What's that noise?" my mom asked him as he rushed downstairs.

"Found it," he yelled from the basement.

He held the witch's mug in his hand. He tilted the hat back. "Hahahahaha," it snickered with laughter. It seemed like Grandma was still in charge of Halloween.

In the spring, my mom visited us in California. We reminisced about Grandma's life, sipping her favorite hazelnut coffee as a tribute.

"I almost forgot. Your grandma wanted me to give you this." Into my palm, she dropped Grandma's wedding ring, the same one she had stopped wearing years before due to the swelling in her hands.

With a trembling chin, Mom said, "You both have slender fingers."

"It's beautiful," I said. "I miss her."

As I held Grandma's wedding ring between my fingers, I remembered doorbells, spider rings, and a mysterious phone call in the night. I know her spirit will always be with us.

STACEY GUSTAFSON is an author, humor columnist, and blogger. Her blog *Are You Kidding Me?* is based on her suburban family and everyday life. Her stories have appeared in *Chicken Soup for the Soul* and *Not Your Mother's Book* series.

Dave's Hug

RENEE STAMBAUGH

My Angel Bump happened a few months ago. I lost my son Dave to suicide in 2016. It has been one of the hardest things I have ever gone through in my life—and I've gone through quite a bit!

One morning I woke after dreaming about him. I looked up toward heaven and said, "Dave, I miss you so much, but I miss your awesome hugs most of all."

I got dressed and went to the market to get a few things. Some days I just need to get out of the house.

When I went to the register, the cashier's name tag caught my eye. His name was Dave! I started to cry. He gently took my hand and asked, "What's wrong?" I said, "My son died from suicide, and this morning I dreamt of him. And when I woke up, I told him I missed him and needed one of his awesome hugs. His name was Dave too. When I saw your name tag just now, it made me cry."

He came out from behind the register and hugged me so hard. I couldn't believe he did that. I thanked him so much for his kindness. By then we were both crying. I walked out of the store and looked up and said, "Thank you, Dave. I will never forget this moment."

Anne Bardsley

RENEE STAMBAUGH is a baby boomer, humor writer, and grandmom of five. She blogs at *The Helpful Hellion*. She is a member of Erma Bombeck's writing group.

Dad's Riding Shotgun

SADIE BENHAM

I am in the process of separation/divorce, and I needed to trade in my car to get something more affordable. If my dad were still alive, he would have guided me. I didn't want to ask anyone else for help or feel like a burden, so I decided to tackle this car buying process alone. While in the car on my way to the dealership, I turned off the radio and started talking to my dad out loud (and I never do this).

I told my dad that I needed his help choosing a car. I asked him to help me so that I don't get ripped off or buy a lemon. I felt more confident after talking with Dad.

A middle-aged salesman approached me, and I told him, "I don't know anything about cars." The salesman asked me why I hadn't brought someone with me. I shared that I had recently lost my dad, was in the separation process, and didn't want to burden anyone. I told him I had a heavenly conversation with my dad. He was going to help me avoid buying a lemon.

"I think I might have a car for you. Your dad just might approve of this one," he said. He reassured me that the vehicle went through a 140-point inspection. After we got back from the test drive, I completed my paperwork and made the purchase!

The salesman came out to the car and paired my phone to the car, and what popped up but "Thomas's iPhone." It was already paired!

I yelled, "Don't delete that! My dad's name is Thomas!" The salesman's jaw dropped. He asked, "Didn't you just tell me you talked to him on the way here? Looks like you got your sign!"

Some people may think it's a coincidence, and maybe so. But in my heart, I know it was my dad! I love and miss him every day, and this made me so happy!

SADIE (SECURRO) BENHAM is a mom of an amazing fifteen-year-old daughter, Sophia. She is a case worker for children who have developmental disabilities. She has a strong passion for helping people.

Baking Bread

MARILYN SMITH

A few years ago, I arrived home from visiting my mom at hospice. She was in a comatose state and near death at age eight-nine. When I got in, it was the middle of the night, so to not wake my husband, I went to sleep in the guest bedroom. Suddenly, I smelled bread baking—the kind my mom used to make with my grandmother.

That particular bread has a very distinctive sweet smell. I was so stunned, I even got out of bed and looked around to see if my husband was baking in the kitchen. But he was fast asleep. No one else was there.

It occurred to me then that my mother was signaling me to let me know she was fine and was passing peacefully into the afterlife.

Years before my mom used to signal me to let me know she got in safely by letting my phone ring twice. I truly believe sending the smell of freshly baking bread was her way of signaling to me that she was going "home" and was safe. I have never experienced anything like this before or afterward.

MARILYN SMITH is a psychologist and lives in Toledo, Ohio.

Anne Bardsley

A Hummingbird's Visit

MEG PRADO

My son, Raphael, was every mother's dream child. He helped at church, sang, and played musical instruments. He was in the choir and theater. He was popular and kind. He helped with the little kid's church group. His smile never left his face.

Raphael was only twenty-one when he had a heart attack. It was a shock to our family and friends. We were devastated. I thought the sun wouldn't shine again after he died. Everyone loved him.

A neighbor asked if she could tell me something one day. We weren't close, so I wondered what she wanted to tell me. She said Raphael had come to her in a dream. "He was all dressed in white, and he lit up the room. He said, 'Please call my mom and tell her that I am okay.' He smiled and repeated his request." I sobbed when I heard her words.

Another day I was inconsolable on the beach thinking about my son. After crying, I decided to take a walk, and I whispered, "I know you can hear me, God. I know you want to tell me he is okay in Heaven. I know it's weak of me to have doubts, but I hope he can hear me in his heart. I want him to have peace in his heart and know he is loved." No sooner had the words left my lips when I looked down to see a heart-shaped stone.

A minute later, I heard a young girl yelling far away at the shore, "Rapha is here, Mom." Rapha is the tender name I used when I wanted to speak quietly with him. I almost fell in the sand, I was crying so hard.

Over the years, more signs arrived. I have always loved hummingbirds, especially the green ones. But I never expected this tiny creature to bring me a sign from my son.

Some days my grief is too heavy for me. On those days, I walk to the stream near the back of my house and listen to the water flowing. It helps me settle. I know my son is with God, and he is loved. I just miss him so much.

On this day, I walked to the stream with a heavy heart. I was telling my son how much I loved him. I sat on a large rock and noticed the sun's reflection in the water. A hummingbird arrived to keep me company. I felt the sweetness of this visit in my heart.

The hummingbird landed on my arm. I stared at his beautiful green feathers. He sat there for a few seconds and then his wings hummed as he fluttered right in front of my face.

It was a soul connection. I knew then that my son was giving me a sign. He'd heard me tell him how much I loved and missed him. He was telling me he was still with me. He even remembered that green hummingbirds are my favorite. They represent healing.

At that moment, I cried and laughed. Thank you, God, for letting me feel the presence of my son. I will visit the stream more often and remember this moment forever. I will love you forever, Raphael.

Anne Bardsley

MEG PRADO lives in Brewster, New York. She loves nature walks, the ocean, and lakes. She enjoys volunteering at the local homeless shelter.

Shawn's Alias

BETSY DUNCAN

Our youngest son, Shawn, will be twenty-eight forever. He passed away on April 15, 2017. He was the sweetest person you'll ever meet. He was a momma's boy. He was a bit of a jokester too.

One evening, we gathered at Shawn's house to play cards. We decided to order pizza. Shawn called and ordered. The girl on the phone repeated his order and said, "Okay, that's for John Bailey." Shawn laughed and said, "Yeah, yeah, I'm John Bailey." Shawn's name is Shawn Berry.

He got off the phone and was joking, saying his alias is John Bailey, and we all laughed. Often afterward, we'd call him John Bailey, just for fun.

After Shawn died, I was struggling. I had to go back to work exactly one week after Shawn's funeral. How could I handle this heavy grief in just one week? I thought I'd be a sobbing mess at my job, but I managed to get through the days. My older son also suggested I find a grief group to help me cope. I took his advice and searched online for a support group near me.

While I was at work, one of the grief groups that I had emailed called me. Such a nice man! He told me all about the group, and we talked about Shawn. We talked for a while and then hung up. A few minutes later though, he called me back and asked me, "Do you know the signs of major depression?" We talked for a few more minutes.

When we hung up for the second time, I attempted to save his number on my phone. He was such a kind person to represent his grief group. I felt like I was led to this group. When I looked at recent calls, the number was for Father John Bailey. Oh my god, Shawn's alias is John Bailey! I cried and cried.

I *knew* it was a sign from Shawn. I knew that somehow, some way, if he could get a message or sign to me, he would. And, oh my god, did he!

I have tears right now writing this. This is just one of many signs he has since sent to me.

I *know* there's an afterlife. How could he get me these signs if, when we pass, we are gone forever? He couldn't— no way!

I know in my heart and soul that we will see our loved ones again. I *know* it. I know Shawn is at peace and still a prankster. I know he's near me, I just miss him more than words could explain. I'm sharing my experiences in hopes of helping others along the way. Hugs to you all.

Betsy Duncan is a believer. She did join the grief group led by Father John Bailey. Her son is smiling in Heaven.

Show Me the Money, Dad

Veronica Nelson

As a young girl, one of my favorite memories was when my father taught me to look at the ground and, like magic, money would appear. I always found pennies and dimes. Looking back, I cherish those memories.

On Father's Day of 2019, I took Dad out for dinner to celebrate. We laughed, cried, and laughed some more. Our conversation got emotional, and as always, one of us would make the other laugh. It was at this point I said to my dad, "If you die before me, can you make sure I find quarters instead of pennies because inflation is real!"

My heart shattered when my dad collapsed just a few weeks later. For the next two weeks, I never left his side at the hospital. When Dad moved to Heaven, quarters began to arrive. Each time, I'd look up and rejoice in all our sweet memories.

Since then, I've taken on one of the most challenging jobs I've ever had—and I've had some tough ones. I accepted a position at USPS as a mail carrier, walking between ten and twenty miles a day. Some days when I'm exhausted, I'll be telling myself I can't do this job when, boom! I'll find a quarter at my feet!

Other times, I'll think to myself, if I find a quarter, that means my dad sees me. Boom! I'll find another quarter. Or if I didn't find one all day, I'll think maybe tomorrow he will send one. Sure enough, I'll be coming out of the grocery store. Boom! There's a quarter.

I had to buy a bigger purple jar because the first one is full. My dad's move to Heaven will be three years in August. I miss him every day. I don't get a penny for his thoughts. Then again, I did remind him of inflation. Love you, Dad.

VERONICA NELSON is a fifty-seven-year-old child at heart. She's finally found the key to life: loving the Lord with all her heart in Bourbonnais, Illinois.

The Good Guys

TERRI ELDERS

Nearly a year had gone by since Ken died. As the anniversary of that sad day neared, I felt lonely and longed for a chat. I wanted to tell him that the neighbors across the way finally painted their house, that I didn't like the current contestants on American Idol, and that his favorite restaurant had slated a lobster fest. Most of all, I just wanted to hear his voice.

Then one morning as I dusted the den, a portrait of two dozen movie buckaroos, ranging from Johnny Mack Brown to John Wayne, caught my eye. Its caption, "All of My Heroes Are Cowboys," had made me grin when he'd first positioned the picture when we moved into our retirement home.

Ken claimed his mom had named him for one of the Western stars in the painting, Ken Maynard. "I'm just glad he was the one she idolized, rather than a couple of the other guys up there. I can't imagine having gone through life as Hoot or Hop-along."

The only song he claimed to know the lyrics to was "Paladin," the theme tune from *Have Gun – Will Travel*, a late '50s TV show later adapted to radio. Whenever that show appeared on one of the many cable channels Ken subscribed to during his last years, he'd record each episode and watch them over and over.

"He's a true hero," Ken explained. "Many of the movie cowboys jump right into a fight, but Paladin first tried to settle disputes without violence whenever he possibly could. He not only had brains, but he also had class. He loved good food, good wine, and sharp clothes."

"Here's the thing about Westerns," he'd said, after watching an episode of *Cheyenne* just days before he died. "Life's uncertain enough just as it is. You don't need any ambiguity in your entertainment. So many of the new movies you watch leave too many questions unanswered. I want everything crystal clear at the end. I want to believe that justice always wins out."

My gallant and gutsy husband had absorbed his diagnosis of pancreatic cancer with what seemed to be an almost heroic grace. As he steadily declined during those last months, he rarely complained and never whimpered.

"I can't tell you how brave I think you are," I'd said.

"Brave? Nah. Just accepting the inevitable," he answered. "Tom Mix wouldn't be boohooing. Neither would Wild Bill Elliott."

Ken tried to be a good guy until the end, I now recalled, finishing the dusting. After I was done tidying the den, I decided I'd settle down to watch a video. I rummaged through some of Ken's old DVDs and paused at one titled *50 Western Classics*.

Then I heard Ken whisper, just as clearly as if he'd been standing in the room next to me: "Did you get a birthday card for Rick?"

I glanced around, and of course, there was nobody else

in the room. Yet I was convinced it had been his voice—his soft inflection, his wry tone.

Oh, heavens, I thought. *He's right!* I realized I'd forgotten Ken's middle son's birthday, which was coming up fast. Instead of watching a DVD, I'd drive to town and get a card. Then I'd stop by the post office for some stamps.

As I entered the post office, I glanced at the display case. The new commemorative stamps, "Cowboys of the Silver Screen," bore portraits of four of the men in Ken's lithograph: William S. Hart, Tom Mix, Gene Autry, and Roy Rogers. All four wore jaunty white cowboy hats. I could almost hear Ken's voice again, reminding me that anybody could tell they were all good guys.

I twisted my mouth into a smile as I approached the counter, even though I had to stifle a sniffle.

"I'll take five sheets of the cowboy stamps," I said, reaching into my purse for a tissue. I blotted a tear from my eye.

The post office worker opened her drawer and counted out several sheets. "Got a spring allergy?" she asked.

"Nope. I'm just overjoyed by these stamps."

"Well, they're certainly cheery," she said, totaling my tab.

"They remind me so much of my husband."

"Whatever." She shrugged and reached for my credit card. She glanced from the stamps to my face and back and then shook her head.

I ducked my head to hide a smirk. *She thinks I'm the odd one,* I thought. *I bet she doesn't know that Paladin's horse was named Tanglefoot or that Tom Mix's was Tony. I bet she thinks Cheyenne is just a city in Wyoming!*

Whether it came from inside or outside of my head, that whispered reminder about Rick's card reassured me that my husband still cared about me. He'd found a way to steer me away from melancholy into happy memories. Long after he'd ridden into his final sunset, Ken still knew how to be a good guy—a hero. I call that a miracle indeed.

Terri Elders has been published in 150 anthologies. She has written feature articles for countless national and international periodicals. A native Californian, Terri has lived and worked all over the world with the US Peace Corps.

The Kiss

MARCIA PETERSON

I finally dreamed about my husband last night after his sudden death seven months ago. He came to me young and perfect, his beard tinged with red as it was when I met him thirty years ago.

He got up real close to my face, and the love we felt was so strong. Right before he kissed me, I said, "Well *there* you are!" When he kissed me, oh my god, it was all the love we felt for each other for over thirty years all wrapped up in one kiss.

I remember other people were around us, and I could hear them thinking, "Wow, now that is a Great Love!" I woke up and just lay there sighing, filled with joy.

It didn't last long, but it could have been an eternity. If I never dream about him again until I die, I will be content. I will hold him, and that kiss, in my heart.

Thank you, God. Thank you.

MARCIA PETERSON lives in Pembroke, Virginia. She enjoys the simple life of a small town in the Appalachian Mountains. She is an RN as well.

The Wind Beneath My Wings

Lee St. John

"I am only living for you," she said the night before she died.

My parents married at thirty. I was their only child, born ten years later. They called me a menopause baby, as Mother never had a chance at having another. And although I was a scamp and they were starting to tire because of the forty-year gap in our ages, they told me I brought joy into their world.

Before Mother babied me, she babied my father for those ten years. When I came along, she babied us both. Once, many years later, Mother and I traveled to Hawaii and San Francisco, as Daddy didn't have any interest in traveling. It was the 1970s, so we did not have a microwave yet. So, before we left on our trip, Mother cooked, labeled, and froze a dinner meal for each night we would be away. For ten days! All my father had to do was take the meal out of the freezer and let it thaw before warming it up. "Nothing says loving like something from the oven."

And she pampered me my whole life too. Criticized by her other mother friends who all had older offspring and "knew best," she was told, "You are spoiling her." Mother always responded, "She's just well-loved."

Daddy died at seventy-one, the year after I married. Mother lived another seventeen more. Growing up, it was a concern of mine that my parents wouldn't last as long as my friends' youthful parents. However, Mother made it to eighty-eight. I think that was pretty good. But I didn't marry young either, and that put her at a double disadvantage. I was thirty-two when my first child was born.

In my mother's last years, I would take her to the doctor with a second son in tow who was born when I was forty. There we were, like the Three Stooges, but ages eighty-four, forty-four, and four. Our conversations went like this while Mother was holding on to her walker: "Mother, hurry up! Baby, slow down! Mother, hurry! Baby, wait up!" And I was sandwiched in the middle.

And Mother needed more attention than I could give. Because of my work, my husband, and my two boys, I realized as time went by that my tender, loving care wasn't enough. I needed help.

We chose a facility that took good care of her. I visited her three times a day. Sometimes I would set my alarm at 2:00 a.m., or at other morning times, to pop in to see her so that the staff didn't count on my routine checks. I shouldn't have worried. They were angels themselves.

While Hubby was out of state during Veteran's Day weekend of 2001 playing golf and watching the Auburn–Georgia football game, I visited Mother and we watched the game on television. She and I both went to the University of Georgia to work toward a master's in education. My hubby went to Auburn.

After the game was over, and not knowing it would be her last night, I loved on my mother, giving her a load of

Anne Bardsley

kisses while saying goodnight. I told her to sleep well and that I would see her in the morning. That's when she said it: she was only living for me.

I received the phone call of her passing around 6:30 a.m.—they had tried to reach me earlier, but I was in a sound sleep and Hubby was not around to hear the phone either.

I left quickly to get over to her room at the health facility. I spoke with the nurse on duty and asked if she could tell me anything about my mother's last moments. She said she had visited Mother's room around 2:00 a.m., and when she returned at 3:00 a.m., Mother was gone.

I started making plans for her funeral. As I was an only child, my beautiful mother was everything to me: mother, neighbor, high school government teacher, friend, sister—she checked all the boxes. She was also a brainiac, and I was a social butterfly. She was diligent, and I was all over the place. As that scamp, she still let me be me. In addition to the traditional Presbyterian service, my cousin sang the Bette Midler title song "Wind Beneath My Wings" from the movie *Beaches*.

I was heartbroken.

A year passed, and here it was Veteran's Day weekend again. Hubby had that Monday off and was playing golf at another out-of-state destination. My mother had died on Sunday, November 11, 2001. This Sunday of the holiday weekend, a year to the day of her passing, I was awakened by what I thought was a gentle noise coming from my husband's side of the bed. Drowsily, I started gaining my senses and realized that music was coming from his nightstand's radio. I looked at the digital clock's time and it read 2:35 a.m. As I sat up, I heard the music coming from the radio—it was the song "Wind beneath My Wings."

How could that be? How could the radio come on suddenly that early on a Sunday morning when it did not any other time? How could it be exactly a year to the day of my mother's death? How would she have known that song was sung at her funeral? She didn't request it, and I doubt she was even familiar with that movie or Bette Midler's songs. And the fourth part of this equation was the time of morning: between 2:00 a.m. and 3:00 a.m. It was a sign for sure. Mother was telling me what I had wondered many times: she died at 2:35 a.m. She was still around.

Crying, I then jumped out of bed and said aloud, "Hey, Mama! We are all okay. Now I know you are."

My faith grew that day. No sermon or religious pronouncements would ever give me that much comfort of an afterlife for us all. This was my special heavenly message as my mother let me know she was still with me as always before—the wind beneath my wings.

This story was previously published in *Chicken Soup for the Soul*.

LEE ST. JOHN is a #1 Amazon Bestseller, a final four nominee for the 2019 Georgia Author of the Year Award in the essay category, an Erma Bombeck writer, and a *Chicken Soup for the Soul* contributor.

Saluting Don's Eagle

CAMY JOYNER

We buried my husband, Don, in a full-honors service at Arlington, Virginia, on August 10. He had a fly-over, the caisson, the Air Force band, Honor Guard, the bugler playing *Taps*, and the 21-gun salute. The service was captured by Arlington Media for prosperity. Don's funeral was stunning.

When I received the photos and video from the media company, I saw something I hadn't noticed at the cemetery: there was an eagle in the sky.

When my dad was buried in 1997, we were all outdoors at the house. My siblings spotted four eaglets between the bluffs making what looked like their first flight. Usually, you didn't see four eaglets at a same time. My sister asked if I thought that meant anything, and I said, "Yes, I think it means that the four of us kids are now flying on our own, and Daddy wants us to fly right." It was one of his favorite warnings to us.

A single golden eagle in Arlington probably just meant the bird lived in one of those big beautiful trees nearby. If it was sighted flying over Don's service, then it could be a sign that he wanted us to know his spirit was with us. He was, after all, a colonel. As you may know, they have nicknames such as "Bird Colonel" or "Full Bird."

When Arlington Media called me to be sure I liked the videos, I asked about the eagle. I held my heart when he said, "Yes, that eagle was flying overhead at the transfer point, just after the transfer. We heard him make a call and I pointed it out to my photographer. I tried to capture it on video, but I couldn't before the cavalcade began. That's a wonderful story about your dad. We don't normally see eagles flying in that part of the cemetery. Some live closer to the chapel."

Don was there with us.

I am glad that I didn't see that eagle at the time the cameraman did. I know I would have lost what little composure I had had left. But now I got to see it and read about how they spotted it.

On December 14, I will be flying back to D.C. Wreaths Across America has a ceremony bedecking Arlington tombstones with Christmas wreaths. I have ordered one for Don, and they asked if I would be able to be there to place it. I plan to look for that eagle while I am there.

I just want more people to trust in what they feel and see. Life is a richer experience that way.

Camy Joyner is an advocate for veterans who have been affected by Agent Orange. She receives signs from Don regularly. He is very creative!

My Handsome Angel

FRANKIE MacCORMACK

Albert and I were married for thirty-six years. My husband loved his family and his church, and he was especially devoted to the Blessed Mother. We had four children in six years. Albert was the strict one. That's the way he was raised. I was more relaxed with the kids. It wasn't always easy disciplining that many youngsters at once.

We had some rough years, but when the children grew up and left home, we had a lot less to disagree about. In 2000, he started to have medical issues. When the doctor's office called him to come in for the results of some biopsies, we were worried.

I asked Albert if he wanted me to go with him. He was very independent, but this time he said, "Yes." We were both shocked to hear of the aggressive nature of the cancer. We left the doctor's office holding hands. Albert said to me, "Well, I have to get my affairs in order."

And that he did. He even told me who he wanted to do the readings and what hymns he wanted at his funeral. He was diagnosed on September 27 and had the surgery in mid-October, but the reports showed it had already spread to his esophagus. They were only able to remove the stomach.

I learned so much about acceptance from Albert. He knew he wasn't going to live but lived each day making a goal for that day. He would try to walk a few steps further, eat a little more.

We prayed together every evening.

He would praise me, telling the palliative care staff that he had the best nurse there is and she was with him 24-7. I was a retired nurse and very fortunate to be able to care for him at home.

His doctor asked him to go to the hospital for more tests. Our children flew in to spend more time with him. My daughters and I stayed with him during his last two nights. We prayed and sang Albert into the loving arms of Jesus. He died in the hospital on December 20 and was buried on December 22.

The funeral was at our parish where Albert had worked. Our pastor broke down during his homily. He told of Albert's devotion to our Blessed Mother. He said he had heard someone talking in the church one day and had come out of his office. It was Albert talking to "Mary."

During Albert's last few weeks at home, he had said, "I'll send you signs that I'm still with you." Then he'd continued to tell me things I'd need to know about the furnace.

After his death, I would go from room to room, thinking about him in tears. One day I sat on his side of the bed. I was alone in the house with my back to the bedroom door, and I felt his large hand on my back. I didn't jump or holler. I just felt peaceful.

The second episode happened one night when I awoke to see a shape in our bed. Again, it wasn't frightening. Half asleep, I thought, "It must be Albert."

After those episodes, I talked to him whenever I needed

help hanging blinds or doing other chores with a hammer or screwdriver.

I still miss him, but I know I have a tall handsome angel waiting for me in Heaven.

FRANKIE MACCORMACK has lived alone for twenty-one years now. She continues to grow in her faith. She has gratefully been a member of Christ Renews His Parish at St. John Vianney in St. Pete Beach as a snowbird for the past eighteen years.

Mother of the Bride Dress

CAROL WALSH

My mother died in 1986, but it was in 2008 that I got the message I needed. It was not the first time I felt her nearness, but it was perfectly timed. I was shopping with my youngest daughter for a mother-of-the-bride dress for me. My oldest daughter was getting married, and we were overjoyed. But these moments in life are so difficult when someone you love should be there.

My young daughter picked out this vibrant pink dress that you might wear to an Academy Awards ceremony. It was simply not my color. But I thought in a less flashy color the dress might work, so I decided to try it on in brown. Then I came out to check it in a mirror and show my daughter. A woman near me said, "It looks nice on you, but do they have it in another color?"

I said, "Yes, they do, but it's in pink."

"Oh, let me see it!" she said excitedly.

I went back in and changed into the pink version. When I came out and looked in the mirror, a very strange feeling came over me. I can't explain it. The woman said, "Oh, that looks just right on you. It's simply beautiful!"

I looked at her and asked, "Can you tell me your name?"

Anne Bardsley

She said, "My name is Rose." I was flabbergasted. With tears in my eyes, I told her, "Rose was my mother's name."

I knew my mother was right there. My daughter agreed that we had an angel with style that day. We laughed and we cried.

Thanks, Mom. I'll see you at the wedding.

CAROL WALSH lives in Long Island, New York. She's a NYC firefighter with Engine 58 in Harlem. She enjoys travel and her family. Life is good.

Lucas Knows

JENNIFER MEYER

This is a reminder to all who need it. When we lose someone close, there will always be some sort of connection to their energy or soul.

My three-year-old son Lucas and his friend were riding with me in the car the other day. My son's friend pulled out an old flashlight from a box in the back seat. I'd been meaning to get rid of it. Lucas had wanted to play with it months ago, but I wasn't able to get the darned thing to work. I had put new batteries in it and still nothing

It has sentimental value, so I couldn't just pitch it at the time. Wanting to see what Lucas's answer would be, I asked his friend to show it to Lucas and ask who it belonged to.

Without hesitation, Lucas responded, "It's Grandpa's flashlight." Lucas asked for it back. His friend handed him the flashlight. As soon as Lucas hit the on-switch, the light shone brightly. It hadn't worked even with new batteries. Now it was a bright beam.

When Lucas was two, I was cleaning out the car my father-in-law had given me before he had passed. I had found out I was pregnant just one week after his passing.

While I was cleaning the car, Lucas said, "Mommy, this is Grandpa's car." He could never have known that. I asked, "How did you know that?"

He said, "He sits right there."

I asked, "You can see him? What does he look like?"

He said, "He looks like me, Mommy." My husband and I didn't think they looked alike, but Grandpa was an older dad. We'd never seen photos of his younger years. After Lucas's remark, we had family members look for old photos.

Sure enough, Lucas was right. The resemblance is undeniable. He's a mini-Grandpa.

Even though we may physically lose someone we hold dear to our hearts, occasionally a light will shine to remind us they are always with us.

Watch for it.

JENNIFER MEYER lives in Mantua, Ohio, with her husband. She has cared for many children; however, she was never able to conceive. One week after her father-in-law died, Jennifer learned she was pregnant. After twenty-five years of trying, she had conceived at the age of forty-three.

Metaphor or Miracle

ANNETTE LANGER

My mother had two oval bars of soap, baby-pink and carved like delicate flower petals, just large enough to hold in one's hand. She tucked away one of them in the closet for safekeeping but displayed the other in a white milk-glass dish shaped like a flat seashell. A small cherub reclined at one side, cradling the edge of the shell. The soap lay beside the little angel, to be admired but never used, like her fancy candles that were "too good" to burn.

After she lost a long, bitter fight with cancer, I faced the task of readying my mom's home for sale. I took the soaps home, putting one decorative bar away as she had and setting the other in its dish on the edge of my kitchen sink. It was the last thing I looked at each morning before work and the first thing I saw when I returned at night. It seemed to symbolize her spirit watching over me. It bridged the gap between us.

The first Thanksgiving after she died was hard. My friend Lois suggested we spend it together, and I offered to make the turkey dinner. It was good to have the company on my first holiday alone. Lois left shortly after dinner, and I busied myself clearing up the dishes. Later, I absently flipped through the TV channels but found nothing interesting, I turned off the television and went to bed.

The next day was back to business as usual. That evening I came home from work and went directly to the kitchen to wash my hands. I glanced at the milk-glass dish—it was empty! *Could I have thrown the soap out with the Thanksgiving dinner scraps?* My stomach clutched for a moment, but I forced myself to relax and reach back into my memory of that morning. I was positive I had seen it there in its dish before leaving for work. I picked through the garbage bags and then rummaged through kitchen cabinets and drawers, just in case. No luck.

I phoned Lois. We reviewed my search efforts, ticking off the places I had looked. Then she asked if I had checked the sink disposal. Cradling the phone with one hand, I held my breath and reached down inside. I touched a mushy oval object languishing at the bottom of the drain. I lifted it out and gazed through my tears at the now unrecognizable shape in my hand that once had been my mother's treasured bar of soap. I couldn't bear to throw it out, even if it was no longer beautiful. I placed it in its glass dish on the counter to dry. There were no words to console me. Tearfully, we said goodbye.

The next morning, I went into the kitchen to make breakfast. I did a double take as my eyes riveted on the once-again-empty glass dish. I thrust my hand down into the disposal but found the drain empty—the soap was gone.

A year slipped by, yet the pain of losing my mom had not lessened; my prayers for release from my sorrow went unanswered. One Sunday I learned that my church offered grief counseling. The facilitator's name was Annette, the same as mine. I took it as a sign to attend.

At the weekly meetings, I listened to each person's sad story, and that depressed me even more. Knowing I wasn't alone didn't help.

There was never any pressure to speak. Annette invited everyone to recount memories of lost loved ones when (or if) they felt ready. I listened halfheartedly, but my thoughts drifted back to my sadness. Then there was silence. Annette allowed it to run its course, speaking just before it became awkward.

Then one night it was I who broke the stillness, ready to tell my story to the group, and it was about the lost bar of soap, of all things. As the details tumbled out, I felt the same helplessness that I did when remembering my mother was alone when she died. Those demons still haunted me—I wasn't with her at the end, *and* I had lost her precious bar of soap. That sounded silly, even to me, but I felt I had failed her twice.

When I finished, no one in the room spoke. Finally, Annette pierced the silence. "You are very close with your mother, aren't you?"—Not "you were close," but "you *are* close." I found that strange but intently took in every word— "Understand that your mother hasn't left you, that she's always with you," she said. "But she needs to be where she is, and you need to be here, where you are. You no longer have to wait to tell her things. You can share with her the instant something happens."

Then Annette focused on the guilt I felt because my mom had died alone. She suggested that perhaps my mother tried to stay alive for my sake because she knew I wasn't ready to let her go. Annette said the one time I wasn't there gave my mother permission to leave.

"I believe the missing soap is a metaphor," she offered.

Anne Bardsley

"Your mother is still speaking to you now. She's saying, 'Wash your hands of this and let go.' She didn't disappear along with the soap. Only her pain disappeared."

It was as if Annette had flipped a switch. In that very instant, my pain ended. At once, I understood, and I accepted it. I could allow my mother to rest in peace, and I was at peace too.

That was the last time I attended grief therapy. I had stopped grieving. My periodic search for the soap ended as well. The remaining bar of soap now resides in its dish on my bathroom vanity, and I can look at it and smile.

I've prayed for many things in life, most of which I haven't received, at least not in the way I had envisioned. But I finally learned to pray the simplest, most powerful prayer of all—"Thy will be done." Now I receive everything I need.

Annette passed away prior to the publication date of this book.

ANNETTE LANGER was a kind soul with a servant's heart. She volunteered over eight thousand hours with the Pleasanton Police Department in California. She was also a talented humor writer. Her work was featured in four of the *Chicken Soup for the Soul* series. She authored several books. She was loved.

It's All About Change

BETTE BAKER

I was raised in a loving home, yet my parents were two entirely different people. My mother was the enforcer, and my dad was the forgiver. When I reached that stage in life where I started to make my own decisions, my mother became much tougher on me than she was on my two brothers. I always figured it was because I was the only girl and the middle child. She loved me, but I didn't know how much until she passed away.

Not long after she passed, I started finding coins, usually pennies, but then there were nickels, dimes, and quarters. It took me a while to figure out that the coins were always tails up. Then I realized that I only found them when something was weighing heavily on my heart, or I was going through a tough life decision.

The greater my stress and burden, the higher the denomination of the coin. It was my mother sending me her love and letting me know she was sharing my burden and praying that whatever I was going through, it would all work out for the best.

Dimes would be found on a freshly made bed two minutes after I walked out of the bedroom when I was home alone. A nickel, the day my granddaughter moved into her dorm room as a freshman in college. A dime in the dryer with a load of throw rugs? There are no pockets in throw rugs, for the love of Pete! A dime in the pocket of a brand new, just purchased pair of jeans.

Pennies in mud puddles beside my car door. I mean, Mother…a mud puddle?

These coins from my mom have made a huge "change" in my life and have helped me immensely in mending my heart from some hurtful events that occurred between us.

Keep sending me the coins, Mom. I am saving for a trip to see your beautiful face.

BETTE BAKER lives in Millersburg, Pennsylvania. She loves the beach and the sun. Her granddaughter, Skylar, is the joy of her life.

High Hopes

VIOLET MULHERN TURNER

My Italian-born mother came to America after World War II destroyed her village. Even though the family cemetery plots were two hours from home, she often wanted to go. I would drive her and my daughters there, and she'd make a day of it: visiting the nursery, planting on the graves, taking my girls to the food truck outside, and buying them candy. When she died, I'd go several times a year to plant.

One time there alone, it occurred to me that other than a pressing on my back—indigestion or my mom, who knows—there'd been no sign from her. I planted, pruned, sat on her grave, and said, "If anyone would have found a way to send a sign it was you, but nothing. Okay. I guess when you're dead, you're dead." As I left, in a *Monty Python* moment, I blasted Frank Sinatra's "High Hopes," a song my mother loved, from my car with the windows down, and sang along.

The next day I went for a routine mammogram. I checked in, sat, and read, waiting to be called. The receptionist approached me. She looked reticent, and I was convinced they'd found something. This wouldn't be good. She said, "I'm sorry to bother you, and I never do this, but I just have to ask…" Yup! Here it comes! The end is near. She was literally tearing up, which made me start.

But she said, "Are you Rita Mulhern's daughter?" I told her I was. It was odd, since my married name is Turner. How had she known? She said, "When I check people in, I glance at the name but never the address. This time, for some reason, I looked. Please don't think I'm a stalker or anything, but my son and I were driving around your mother's neighborhood yesterday. I told him that his grandmother—do you remember, Louise?"

I told her yes, Louise was my mother's coworker. She had been at my mother's funeral.

"So, I told him Grandma was friends with a lady who lived in this house. We even drove around the creek to see if the houseboat was still there, and when it was, I said, 'I bet her daughter lives there now.' I told him about Rita's artwork and gardening, and I never look at addresses, but I looked at yours, and so, I don't know, I thought it might be sign."

We were both sobbing. When I left the office, I called my husband and explained that I was going back to the cemetery. As I pulled in, a song I wrote that a friend had recorded was playing on my radio. I paused the player, parked, and had a good talk and a long cry with my mother.

And when I started the car, "High Hopes" was playing.

VIOLET MULHERN TURNER was raised in Brooklyn and Long Island. She wrote for radio and print. She taught prison inmates creative writing. She was a high school teacher for over thirty years.

Grandmom Knows

Rose Gazzara

I had a very special bond with my maternal grandmother growing up. She was such a sweet woman. And I loved her with all my heart. She became my angel when I couldn't conceive, praying daily that my husband and I would have a baby. She was convinced that God had a child planned for us.

We wrote back and forth to each other from Puerto Rico. Her faith was so strong. She knew in her heart we would conceive, but I wasn't so sure it would ever happen. It took four years before I was finally pregnant with my son. I was overjoyed! After that, my grandmom and I prayed that my husband and I would have a healthy child.

We talked incessantly about how wonderful it would be to finally hold that little bundle of blessings. Unfortunately, my grandmom died before our son was born. I wish she had been at his baptism when we christened him Louis. He was a happy, healthy baby. He often giggled as he stared into space. I'm convinced my grandmom was entertaining him.

About three months after Louis was born, I went to a birthday party. My girlfriend's mother-in-law was holding my son. I asked her to let me take a picture of them. When I focused the camera, I saw my grandmom holding my son!

Anne Bardsley

I ran around the yard crying uncontrollably. My grand-mom did see my son. She was holding him, just as we had talked about. My heart was so happy. All of her prayers were answered. Mine were too.

She visited me once again. We decided to try to get pregnant again when Louis was one. Since we had such a difficult time, we knew it might take some time again. Two miscarriages followed, and we were devastated once more. After many doctor's visits, we decided maybe Louis would be an only child. We accepted it that day.

After five years, I missed a period. My husband insisted I buy a pregnancy test. I was doubtful, but I bought the test. The morning I took the test and watched it wick up to a positive result.

Oh my god, I'm pregnant! I was elated but also scared. The last two miscarriages were so difficult. I didn't think I could go through another one. And then I heard the words, "Yes, you are pregnant, and it's a girl!"

I froze. I was all alone in the bathroom. The voice was loud and clear as if someone was standing right beside me.

I knew in my heart it was my grandmom. It seemed she had already met our daughter.

ROSE GAZZARA lives in New Jersey. She is enjoying life as a grandmother herself now.

Ghost Rider

WALTER CRAFT

On Mother's Day, I was traveling to my mother's grave. It was just after dinner and still daylight, with good visibility and a nice clear road. I was heading west on a rural highway and passed a sheriff's deputy heading east. He immediately pulled off the road and spun around behind me. I sensed he was pulling me over but was confused why. I was not speeding. My Jeep was brand new, so I knew my taillights weren't out. Nonetheless, when he flashed his lights, I pulled right over.

The officer approached my car and seemed very agitated. He quickly asked me, "Where did he go?" I kind of laughed and said, "Where did who go?" I was traveling alone, so I was puzzled about who he was referring to. He said, "Your passenger, he wasn't wearing a seat belt."

At this point, he had a very concerned look and had placed one hand over his gun while he stepped back from my car and started to look in the back windows with his flashlight. I was very calm and assured him I was indeed alone and was traveling to put some flowers on my mother's grave. He simply couldn't have seen a passenger in my car. After he thoroughly checked my car, he stated that he saw me pull over and knew no one had fled my car, yet he was so confused because he truly thought he had seen someone. So I humored him. I asked, "What did my ghost rider look like?"

I never could have been prepared for his answer. He said, "It was a teenage boy, with bright curly red hair." I instantly got chills as I told him that he had just described my son, Wally. My son had died in a tragic drowning accident five years ago, when he was fifteen. One of our favorite things to do was drive around and listen to music.

I would've loved to believe my son was riding around with me. The truth was though that I hadn't felt any presence at all. The officer laughed it off and joked about getting his eyes checked the next day, but it has made me wonder so much about that night. Could he have seen my son's spirit with me? Of all the people he could have described, he had described my Wally!

When life feels heavy and I need some tranquility, I visit the place where he died. This spot is a canal under a bridge in upstate New York. It's very peaceful. I stopped the other day to take a breather and noticed there was a lot of debris in the water, mostly tree branches from a recent storm.

Just as I was about to leave, I glanced down and saw some sticks that had formed the words "Hi Dad." It was clear and right in front of me. As soon as I saw it, the sticks separated and floated down the canal. That day I felt his presence so strong.

My son is very creative with his signs. I was sitting in my garage one day, the door open, and a cardinal flew in and landed on a box behind me. I thought this was a cool nature moment. Then he flew away. He flew back through the door a minute or two later and landed on my shoulder. He perched there for ten seconds or so. I froze. I was afraid if I moved, I would startle him, and he might attack me. I just sat still, looking at this beautiful bright red bird sitting just three inches from my face.

When he flew away again, I ran inside and told my wife. She mentioned that it could have been a sign. I realized my red-headed son sent a red-winged cardinal to visit me.

Each of his signs is different. I never know when one will arrive. I do know that my heart overflows with love each time.

WALTER CRAFT lives in Schuylerville, New York. He enjoys time with his family and the outdoors.

Escorting Dad Home

SHARON HIGSON

M y dad had been sick for quite a while. And like many others, my mom was his caregiver. She took him to doctor appointments, did all the leg work, and just looked after him in general. His health wasn't great. He had blocked arteries in his legs and neck, which required surgery. He had prostate cancer but beat it after thirty-seven trips to the hospital; my mom drove most of the time to these distant appointments. To add to that, he ended up with an aortic aneurism.

As life would have it, Mom passed away before Dad. She went to bed one night and never woke up. Both sides of the family were shocked as she had never shown any signs of illness. Dad remained behind. So in and out of the hospital he went. His blood pressure would drop and he would hit the floor, bruising badly. We were so worried about him, but he wanted to remain at home.

This went on for five months. He had to be left alone all day because my brother, who lived with Mom and Dad, worked full time. My kids were teenagers at the time, in need of me in their lives, and I worked part time; we also lived thirty-five minutes away, on a good traffic day.

As all of this was going on, my family and I were getting the paperwork sorted for our upcoming move to Australia. Things got stressful. My brother and I argued, Dad felt like we were pushing him to go into a long-term care facility, and there was no resolution for anyone. I was becoming a big mess.

After another trip to see Dad in the hospital an hour's drive away, I lost it. I was standing in front of my kitchen window, sobbing, alone, and quite distraught. And then it seemed to just appear.

There were no other clouds in the sky that I could see. And this one was quite significant. It was shaped like a giant hawk (which has since become my totem). And then my mother's face appeared in it.

The greatest sense of peace washed over me, like a blanket of tranquility. I felt cleared of all my stress, relieved and safe. I heard her voice in my head, telling me it was all going to be okay.

With the help of the doctors from the hospital, we managed to get Dad into a long-term care facility, and my family and I moved to Australia. Eight months later, my son and I were back in Calgary for a friend's wedding. It had been a long flight, but I was up for a get-together with my mom-in-law and friends. We stayed up way too late, and at 2:00 a.m., I went to bed filled with wine and good cheer.

At 5:00 a.m., my brother phoned to let me know my dad was in the hospital again. His aneurysm had burst and there was nothing they could do.

When I arrived at the hospital, my brother left to get some rest, and I settled into a comfy chair the nurses brought me. It could take days for Dad to pass through this agony, and they had given him morphine. He was often wrestling, whether in pain or waging a war within himself, it wasn't clear. Once he looked right at me, and I hoped he knew I was there.

I was jet-lagged and half-asleep in the chair with my eyes closed when it felt as if someone had entered the room. There was a sudden energy change. I sat upright and looked toward my dad, to the right of him—I knew it was my mom standing beside him. She had come to comfort him one last time. Maybe she had come to comfort me as well.

I have felt her presence, as well as other members of my family, a few times since. I am a strong believer that we are watched over, protected, and loved so maybe we can carry messages of love and strength to others.

SHARON HIGSON, at the age of sixty-three, is a student of energy healing and life and a retired article writer. She lives with her husband and two cats in the region of Queensland, Australia.

Daddy's Little Girl

CAROL BERTOLUZZI

It will be my dad's first anniversary in Heaven this week. He must have known how hard this is for me. I miss him, his smiling face, his tender ways, and his "I love you, take care" farewells. I was the little girl who would look out the window every day as she waited for her daddy to come home from work. When his car pulled into the drive, I'd run out to greet him with a big hug. I just loved my daddy.

At ninety-five, he looked and acted like he was sixty. No one could believe he was that old. His driver's license was renewed at ninety-five. I imagined him in line with a bunch of teens taking their driver's test. He was that sharp.

He still cooked his signature dishes of spaghetti, split pea soup, and polenta. He added pork chops to the list toward the end of his life. I can barely write the words "toward the end of his life." I still feel him near me.

Dad loved everyone. He was a greeter at church for years. He was proud to welcome people into the church. He stood tall and handsome. I can still see his smile.

My parents celebrated their seventieth wedding anniversary while my mom was in a nursing home. He couldn't hold his bride or kiss her due to COVID-19 isolation. Their love was a match made in Heaven.

My dad loved kids. He was so gentle that kids reacted to him easily. He influenced many kids in his lifetime. When he was a Sunday school teacher, he invited his class to go camping. He could have been the Pied Piper!

The day my dad entered Heaven, I was waiting for the morticians to arrive at the house. As they entered the room, I asked my dad for a sign that he'd never be far from me in spirit. There was a framed photo on a shelf. I'd no sooner spoken those words when the framed photo flipped itself over. The mortician looked at me and said, "Well there's your answer!" I smiled and I cried.

My dad's favorite musician was Glen Miller. His favorite song was "In the Mood." I was driving in my car with my usual '70s music blaring when suddenly Glen Miller was belting out "In the Mood" in my car. My dad must have been sitting shotgun that day. I still can't figure out how that happened.

Another unexpected sign came soon after. I was walking toward my condo when I spotted a glass heart on a tree. I swear it wasn't there the day before. It felt like my dad was telling his baby doll, as he called me, "I love you and take care." I smiled and cried again.

One day I was especially missing my dad. I feed my mom in the nursing home twice a day, and some days my heart is so sad. But I love my time with her, and I'd never change a thing. On my way home, I happened to look to the left, and there was a cloud formation that looked like an angel. I couldn't pull over to get a picture of it. I knew it was my dad telling me he was there with me and Mom.

I guess you could say I was Daddy's little girl. I still am. I love you, Dad. Take care.

CAROL BERTOLUZZI lives in St. Petersburg, Florida. She currently helps take of her mom who lives in a nursing home and has had Alzheimer's for the last ten years.

Baby Shower from Heaven

ANNE BARDSLEY

It was a warm, sunny day in St. Petersburg when I drove our dog, Miss Mattie, to the vet. This day, the top of my convertible was down as Miss Mattie hung out the window to see herself in the side mirror. The COVID-19 virus protocol was that the tech would come to the car and take the animals into the exam rooms while the owners waited patiently outside in the parking lot.

One gentleman next to me struck up a conversation, introducing himself as Bill. He admired my beach buggy blue car. He was retired, a widower, and loved his pooch. I told him I was an author, married forty-three years, and loved my pooch. When he asked what type of writing I did, I told him about Angel Bumps. I explained that I had collected stories from around the world about signs people had received from someone in heaven. He laughed out loud.

"Have I got a story for you!" he said with a big grin. I can't tell you how much I love when someone tells me they have a story. We both got out of our cars to chat. I leaned on my car as Bill told me about his wife, Janet. She'd been battling cancer for two years. Her prayer was that she would live to see her first grandchild be born. She joyfully planned the baby shower, but she passed away before the date.

A few weeks went by, and Bill and his younger daughter, Jill, were out shopping for baby shower gifts. The little one was due in less than a month. Thoughts of how happy his wife would have been buying little dresses and bonnets made him so sad. If only she could have held on another month or two, she'd have been there with them today enjoying this shopping spree.

For some reason, he and Jill both felt compelled to buy a stuffed elephant with the softest big ears. They giggled as the salesclerk put the pink and purple animal in a big bag. In the next department, they purchased little rompers, again with an elephant design. "What is with us and elephants today, Dad?" his daughter asked.

After this, Jill found tiny sleeping gowns and some more rompers. She also found itsy bitsy baby slippers to match. Then a pale lavender and pink quilt caught her eye. "Dad, we have to buy this! There's a sweet baby elephant in the center!"

Bill discovered tiny shorts that were the size of his hand. They were bright pink with a frilly top. When he turned the hanger to see the front, guess what was on the bib of the outfit. Yes, a pink elephant with her trunk up in the air.

They giggled at the size of the clothing. "How tiny will this baby be?" Jill laughed.

Jill wandered into the baby furniture aisle. She touched a white cradle, and he saw her wipe a tear. He said, "I almost cried myself. I put my arm around her and we stood staring at the cradle rocking back and forth."

"Mom would have loved this, Dad," Jill said. It was true. More than anything she had wanted to be here for their first grandchild. "I'm so sad she won't be there." she said. "She was so excited to see this baby. It breaks my heart." Bill gazed over his daughter's head, hoping she'd miss the tears in his eyes.

All they needed now was a huge gift bag to stuff with the sixteen tiny gifts.

Standing in front of the party bag display, Bill said, "How are we supposed to choose one? There must be hundreds here."

Just then, from the very tippy top of the display, a huge purple and pink bag dropped to the carpet in front of them. When they picked it up, they were in shock. On the front of the bag was a beautiful baby elephant surrounded by baby birds and flowers. They stared at each other. "I think Mom just finished our shopping for us. I didn't even see this bag. It was up so high. She must have been with us this entire trip. She's the one who chose the elephant theme for us," Jill said. Then she burst into tears.

Bill hugged his daughter. They were both in tears when the saleswoman asked if she could help them.

"No thank you," Bill said wiping his eyes. "My wife has given us all the help we need today."

"Oh, I didn't see your wife with you," she said, as she looked around curiously.

Jill piped in, "My mom is in Heaven. And today she was right here with us, picking out gifts for my sister's baby."

The woman smiled. "Your mom has great taste." Before we could put our bag and tissue paper on the counter, she commented, "Every little girl needs an elephant."

"How do you know it's a girl?" Jill asked.

The woman smiled and said, "We moms know things."

I just love when people share these stories with me. It warms my heart and makes my eyes leak. How blessed am I?

ANNE BARDSLEY is a humor writer. Her work is featured on Erma Bombeck's humorwriters.org site, *Chicken Soup for the Soul* series, *Feisty After 45*, *The Grand Magazine*, *Guideposts* and more. She served as an honored judge for the Erma Bombeck humor contest. She is the author of *How I Earned My Wrinkles*, *Angel Bumps*, *Hello from Heaven* and this current volume.

All in Good Time

ANNMARIE B. TAIT

Though "Daddy's Little Princess" suits some girls, I liked getting my hands dirty way too much for such a fussy title. But I did adore the man and spent my childhood glued to his heels, firmly believing he could do anything and everything. I have four siblings, but whenever Daddy looked over his shoulder, it was always my face looking back.

While other preschoolers sang the verses of "Twinkle, Twinkle Little Star" and chanted nursery rhymes, I went in another direction, favoring such phrases such as "Why, Daddy? How, Daddy?" and, my all-time favorite, "Can you show me, Daddy?" I repeated these questions so frequently that he suggested I might consider a future with the FBI.

Dad made it his business to answer all of my questions, and I now count among my talents the ability to stain wood, rewire a lamp, paint a room, and hone a knife to a razor-sharp edge on a whetstone. Likewise, there isn't a home improvement contractor on the planet that can pull the wool over my eyes.

During the last two years of his life, as he declined, Dad still strapped on roller skates and plunged full speed ahead. Still, when I saw him settled in his easy chair, baseball cap in place, all was right with the world, no matter how gray his pallor or shallow his breathing.

When the end came, I stoically plodded through the wake and funeral Mass. All of it made sense in my head, but my heart was a ship adrift without a lighthouse in sight.

After he was gone, I visited Mom more frequently, and eventually, we began sorting through Daddy's belongings. When she came upon his watch, Mom handed it to me. "You take this, Annie. I know you will appreciate having it someday." She placed the watch in my hand and my fingers closed around it.

Immediately I recalled Daddy descending the living room steps every morning while slipping the watch over his calloused hand and adjusting it to a comfortable position.

"Thanks, Mom," I squeaked, trying not to cry.

I placed Daddy's watch on my wrist. Its large luminous dial and extra wide band looked comical on me. I didn't care. He wore it every day, and I resolved that I'd wear it every day too. And there it stayed, no matter the occasion or ensemble. When I went to bed, I'd slide my arm under the pillow and listen to the rhythmic *tick, tick, tick* that eventually lulled me to sleep.

On the first anniversary of Dad's passing, I noticed the watch had stopped at the exact time of his death—5:17 p.m. It occurred to me that this might be Dad's way of telling me it was time to move on, and I placed the watch in my jewelry box.

Over the next several months, we gave away or sold most of the furnishings, readied the house for sale, and found a new place for Mom to live in a residential retirement community. She looked forward to making new friends.

I didn't realize it at first, but slowly the cloud of grief

began to lift. The heart-wrenching memories of Dad's final pain and suffering gave way to reminiscing with Mom about happier days. Often, we ended up in a fit of laughter recalling one incident or another.

Still, I'd never lost someone so close, and I realized one day that what I wanted more than anything was to know he was happy even though he'd moved on. I prayed often for his peace and happiness but just accepted that I'd never know for sure. The little girl with all the questions had one that would remain unanswered.

Mom was well settled into her new life and carrying on as best she could when we neared the second anniversary of Dad's departure. I hadn't thought of the watch in months. Then one day I came across it in my jewelry box. I picked it up and discovered to my astonishment that not only was it running but it was also keeping good time, right down to the correct date. Can you imagine? How could that be? It had stopped cold right on the very first anniversary of his death. I'd looked at it a few times since and the time and date had never changed.

Now on the brink of Dad's second anniversary, the watch was keeping perfect time. You might think this was just another odd coincidence, and I might have agreed except for one thing: Dad's watch ran perfectly, never losing a minute, for the next ten years. Watch batteries just don't have that kind of longevity.

Mom was right. I do treasure Dad's watch. In his own good time, Dad answered my final question. When that timepiece came roaring back to life long after it had stopped, Daddy was letting me know loud and clear, "Don't worry about me, Annie, I couldn't be happier."

Of this I have no doubt.

ANNMARIE B. TAIT is newly retired and lives in Harleysville, Pennsylvania, with her husband. She writes stories about her large Irish family. She loves to cook, crochet, and record Irish American folk music with her husband.

A Toast to My Friend

SHYA GIBBONS

Once in a lifetime, you might meet someone who will forever change your life. That person, for me, was A. He was beautiful and a constant reminder of what optimism, love, and acceptance are all about. Our friendship began in a rather unorthodox way: by carrying two PVC pipes and a large banner in a Memorial Day parade. We were chosen to be the representatives for the small-town paper where we worked. I was a journalist, and he was a photography intern; he would later carry on becoming an accomplished, awarded photographer.

After that fateful day, we became close. He was the one who encouraged me to go on my first date with my husband. He was the one I trusted enough to capture the day my husband and I traded vows. We had our silly inside jokes. One time I wondered out loud if I could be a photographer. He instantly handed me his camera and sat patiently while I messed with the settings to take what I was certain would be an artsy, beautiful photograph. It turned out to be a slightly blurry photo of a heating vent. After that, we would randomly send each other photos of heating vents.

Over the years, we drifted apart. We would still get together now and then for a beer, but we were at two different spots in life. When I found out A. had died, I collapsed into a sobbing mess on the floor. The lapse between our get-togethers weighed heavily on my heart.

One night, I couldn't sleep and decided to look through all of our old messages to each other. I thought by going through the messages, it would feel like we were suspended at a point in time when he was still here.

The messages between us went back and forth. I'd apologize for not reaching out sooner, apologize that I didn't know his cancer was back, and express how I wanted to be there for him. He would respond by saying he also could have reached out to me, and that I had no reason to apologize. He knew I'd always be there for him if he called me, any time, day or night.

On the anniversary of his death, I bought a bottle of champagne. My husband and I rarely drink, but it felt like it was a good night to toast our friend's memory. We both poured a small amount and toasted A. Later, I went outside to look at the stars.

Remembering A's fascination with anything Halloween, I brought two Halloween champagne flutes outside. The flutes were thin with a skeleton hand holding the cup part of the glass. I poured some champagne into my flute and some into a flute for A. Then I sat in the grass and spoke to him.

At first, it felt silly, sitting alone outside, crying, and talking to the stars, but then I realized it was exactly what I needed. First, I told him how much I loved and missed him and that I truly hoped he knew I loved him. Then the tears came, which I know he would have hated. Anytime in the past when I had cried as he had updated me on things, he'd tell me to stop because it was okay and to not worry.

I began wiping tears off my cheeks while laughing because I knew that he'd be the first one to tell me to knock off the crying and be strong.

With the flute raised, I said, "I'm not sure what else to say. I'm not going to say goodbye, because it's not goodbye. I know I'll see you again. I'll hear your laugh in my dreams. I'll see a heating vent and your smile will pop into my head. So, I guess I'll leave it simple and say 'I love and miss you.'"

At that exact moment, on this clear night, a strong gust of wind came out of nowhere and toppled A.'s flute over, spilling the champagne out completely. I raised my flute higher, smiled, and said, "Cheers, bud."

I felt his spirit there. I know he was the one responsible for knocking over the champagne flute at the exact moment I tried to toast him. I know that he will continue to drop into my dreams to save me with his laugh. I know there are countless other ways he will visit me.

Now, as I sit outside under the stars again, finishing this piece, I look up to the sky and see one star shining more brilliantly than the rest. He's here. He's watching over me and making sure I'm okay, just like he always did.

SHYA GIBBONS is a stay-at-home mom. She manages her blog *Vintage Dreams with a Modern Twist*. She is happily married and the author of *I Just Want to Be Perfect* and *You Do You*.

A Butterfly's Visit

CHRISTA RYDLEWSKI

I knew Mom's sign would be a butterfly…

My mom was dying of lung cancer. She was eighty-seven years old and said she lived a happy and good life and no longer wanted to go through treatments. Friday, May 4, is when my dad chose to put her into hospice care at home. She wasn't able to talk but turned her head when she heard your voice. Eventually, she wasn't responsive at all and was in a coma-like state.

On May 5, we had a funeral home representative come over to the house so that my dad and I could pick out a urn. We were sitting in the living room. My dad and the rep were on the couch with their backs to the big living room window. I was sitting on a footstool facing them and the window. My dad was drawn to a particular urn that was blue cloisonné with butterflies on it. I loved it! It was beautiful. Just as my dad told the rep, "This is the one," a monarch butterfly slowly flew in front of the window.

One of my friends, who is an empath, said at this point, "Your mom is half here and half in Heaven. She was an extraordinarily strong spirit." I knew then that my mom would visit me often as a monarch butterfly!

On May 9 in the early morning hours, she passed away. The hospice nurse that came over when she passed was wonderful. And when she walked past me, I noticed that she had a butterfly tattoo! Later that morning, my dad and I went to the funeral home to finalize the paperwork. When we pulled into the parking lot and got out of the car, a monarch was flying near us. When we left the funeral home, as we were walking down the sidewalk to the parking lot, a monarch flew in front of us again.

Later that afternoon, my dad had a doctor's appointment, so my son and I ran errands for him. My dad left through the garage at the back of the house. My son and I left through the front door. As we walked down the sidewalk, a monarch flew in front of us and then suddenly flew fast down the side of the house toward the garage. I've never seen a butterfly fly that fast. (It's my thinking that she knew my dad was leaving the garage and wanted to see him go too.)

I stayed with my dad for a week after my mom died. On the fourth day of staying with him, I went home to get some more clothes as I only live about fifteen minutes away. When I pulled into my driveway and got out of my car, a monarch was flying near me once more. As I walked up the driveway toward my house, this monarch flew right beside me. When I got to my front door, it then flew away over the top of my house. I know it was mom, making sure I was okay. And I was, after seeing this monarch follow me.

After staying with my dad for the week, I went back home. Right outside my front door, in front of my living room window, I have ferns. When I got home that evening, I noticed a monarch on one of the leaves of the fern. I stared at it for the longest time and said, "I miss you and love you, Momma." I then took a picture. It didn't move the entire time. The next morning, I went outside, curious to see if it was still there, and it was! I cried, but I was so happy. By the afternoon it was gone.

Later, I went to visit my dad and we had lunch. After running errands and then shopping for groceries for dinner, I went back home. My mind was set that I wouldn't see that monarch again. That it would be impossible for it to be there again two days in a row. Wrong! That same monarch was back! It was in the ferns but on a different leaf.

Momma's strong spirit continued to send signs. Every holiday she used to say, "Don't spend your money on me. I don't need anything." Mother's Day was just four days after my mom's passing, and I was an emotional mess. My son, a police officer, ended his shift early and soon arrived with two flower arrangements. One for me, and one for his grandmom. "These were free, but I swear I was going to buy you flowers after work. Let me explain.

"I was driving down the road and my computer alerted me to a car in front of me. It was a stolen car. The driver was a woman making three flower deliveries. She'd had a family dispute and took a family member's car who reported the car stolen. She was arrested. When I called the flower shop to see if they wanted to arrange delivery, they said to keep them or throw them away. I gave one to the other officer on the scene and kept the other two.

"How funny is it that I was going to buy flowers after work and then on the way home I arrested someone for delivering flowers in a stolen car?"

I laughed and said, "Remember what Grandma always said, 'Don't spend your money on me. I don't need a thing.'"

Seems she doesn't need a thing in Heaven either. Love you, Mom.

CHRISTA RYDLEWSKI lives in St. Petersburg, Florida. She loves butterflies and cherry blossoms. She is a very proud mom of a police officer.

A Winged Visitation

KATHLEEN GEMMELL

"When angels visit us, we do not hear the
rustle of wings, nor feel the feathery touch of
the breast of a dove; but we know their presence
by the love they create in our hearts."

—MARY BAKER EDDY

"Did you know," asked my father when I was a child, "that there are angels amongst us? They may not look like the quintessential ones, wings, halos, and so on. Angels can take many forms."

My father was a beloved family member and friend to many. When he passed, there was standing room only at his funeral. Dad was a kind, humorous, and outgoing man. He was always ready to lend a hand, and I was proud to be his beloved daughter.

I was raised in the Catholic Church and watched my father competently fulfill the role of deacon. He sang in the choir, and Father Joseph visited our home often as he and Dad were buddies. My mother and brother were also steeped in the faith. Christmas, Easter, and Lent were times of joy and spirituality. Every bed in our lovely home had our Savior on the cross above it. I adored the Lord from a young age.

My mother explained that all people have guardian angels. She went on to say that we may not recognize our angels, but they are always there. I found much solace in that as I grew, and from time to time, I would call on my angel for guidance.

My teen years became tumultuous, and I chose, as a rebellion of sorts, to leave the Church when I turned eighteen. My parents were heartbroken. I married an atheist, and we delighted in debating the topic of religion with our friends. Interestingly, although I talked the talk, I still felt a connection to Christianity, even if muted.

As an egotistical young woman, I cared not that my parents suffered. I recall saying to them, "When science proves a higher power created heaven and earth and mankind, I will look at this issue once again." Oh, but my ignorance and self-righteousness were ruling my life.

Believing that my choice was most painful for my father, I tried to make it up to him in other ways. I was a good student and was kind and thoughtful. Yes, my father still adored me, and I, him. I know that my parents prayed for my salvation and went so far as to have Father Joseph speak to me. "Faith is believing in things we can't understand or see. I feel confident that Jesus loves you and that one day you will welcome him back into your soul." I thanked Father but dismissed his words immediately.

My husband and I divorced, and I was lost. Slipping, I found myself falling into prayer often. I wondered why this was occurring but didn't give it much credence. When my father fell ill with cancer, and I could barely cope. My heart ached all day and night as I watched that horrid disease slowly take him from us. He, of course, wanted to find closure before he died, and we had many late-night talks. He asked me to write his eulogy and share it with him. We then held one another and sobbed.

I stood silently as Father Joseph read my father his Last Rites. I held Dad in my arms as my mother and brother and I watched him sigh one last breath.

Years later, I lived in a condominium in a city. One day, as I passed my front window, I was startled to see an American bald eagle land on a spindly branch. This branch had no earthly business holding that magnificent creature. I was taken aback by that and by the notion that this species was in a congested city.

I stood dumbfounded and stared at him with wonder. At that point, he turned and looked me in the eyes. Truth be told, I was near panic. This was all just too bizarre.

Unable to stop looking at this eagle, I met his stare and felt a connection like no other. Talking aloud, I asked, "Dad, is this you?"

The eagle held his glare, as did I. "Dad, you're here in this form to see me, aren't you?" Tears began to cascade down my cheeks and like a lightning bolt striking, I knew. I knew this eagle was my father, an angel. I dropped to my knees and spoke softly, "Dad, thank you for coming. You are my everything, and you have spoken through your eyes. I love you dearly, and I can feel your love for me."

The angel stayed on that thin branch for about a half hour. I remained on my knees and continued to talk. "Dad, I understand why you are with me today. You've come to guide me to the light of our Lord. Someday my time will come, and I must be with you in heaven. I have been self-centered and conceited. Please forgive me, Dad. Please take my soul with you."

Anne Bardsley

My angel flew off, and I marveled at his flight. Calling Father Joseph, I told him of this visitation. He came to my home that afternoon, and we talked. I continued to weep, but my salty tears were from the picture in my mind's eye of that eagle.

"I believe that angels watch over us. I also believe that your father came to you to deliver a message," Father Joseph whispered. "What will you do with that message?"

"I don't know yet, Father, but I truly feel Dad's spirit in my heart. May I come to confession and then attend mass?"

"Your father will be joyful," he answered.

Ten years have passed. I adore eagles and have taught myself about their behaviors. My Catholic soul is readily intact once more.

I have told this story to a few people. Two felt I was delusional, and three believed my father *had* come to me. Regardless of others' opinions, I believe.

Godspeed, Dad. I await your next visit.

"If we never had the courage to take a leap of faith, we'd be cheating God out of a chance to mount us up with wings like eagles and watch us soar."—Jen Stephens

---

KATHLEEN GEMMELL adores the written word. Penning for an array of magazines and anthologies, she is also an animal welfare proponent, a storyteller, and a psychology buff.

Candle Lights and Gardenias

LOIS AND ASHLEY HENRY

I keep a candle burning 24/7 on a memorial table I have designated for my mom. It is battery operated, and when the batteries die, I simply replace them, and it continues to stay lit. It was a few days before my birthday and the batteries had died, but when I went to replace them, the candle would not light. We tried several brands of batteries, but nothing worked.

I thought maybe I needed to replace the candle itself. It had been shining bright for five years. I added it to my list of things to do. Unfortunately, a few days had to go by before I could get to the store. My son even brought over new batteries thinking he could surely get the candle to shine. It wouldn't light up for him either.

Then a few days later, I woke up and the candle was lit! It just so happened to be my birthday. My mom sent me a unique Happy Birthday gift from Heaven. I am loved.

My daughter, Ashley, also has a story about her grandma:

I was very close with my grandma. She passed in June. My first Christmas without her was a very sad time, to say the least. My husband called my mom to let her know I was struggling. He asked if she had some free time to spend with me.

Mom surprised me at my job, and we spent the day together. Appetizers and a drink with Mom cured my sullen mood. A visit to the cemetery was in order and then back to my house. We had a nice time together.

When I walked my mom out to her car at the end of the night, a floral fragrance stopped us dead in our tracks. We went back and forth on what type of flower it might be and then we finally realized it was gardenia. But there were no gardenia plants nearby or even gardenia trees in our neighborhood.

Later that night, my husband and I went for a drive and the fragrance was still outside. I asked, "Do you smell that? This was the fragrance when I walked my mom out to her car." He said, "Do me a favor and google 'the spiritual meaning of gardenias.'"

The first spirit explanation was "a grandmother visiting her granddaughter to tell her she's okay." I had goosebumps and tears. Grandma was sending me a message!

My heart was much happier after that day with my mom. I bet Grandma was smiling when I received her message. Grandma's love has healing powers.

LOIS HENRY lives in Parish, Florida. She's a special education teacher in Manatee County School district. She is married with three children and six grandchildren. Her daughter, ASHLEY HENRY, lives in St. Petersburg and has three children. She is also a special education teacher, in Pinellas County.

My Goodnight Kiss

DAWN REYNOLDS

My father worked as a petroleum engineer for Continental Oil Company. His job required him to travel a five-state area, mostly by car, sometimes by plane. He was gone more than he was home. Dad was a quiet, self-proclaimed "nerd," who loved airplanes, foreign cars, nature, and God. He brought us up to believe that while achievements were nice, showing compassion and kindness were more important than any title or award.

I have often described him as being the most patient man in the world, but as I grew into adulthood, I recalled a couple of instances when he was not exactly exemplary in this regard. Maybe it was because he was so patient with me, as I was his youngest and perhaps most trying child, that I saw him in this light.

While I recall the heartache of saying, "see you real soon," so many times as he headed off on another business trip, I knew he loved me. We had a special bond.

When he returned from each trip, he would often bring a small trinket for me. On one trip, he brought home a nightlight shaped like a little mouse holding an umbrella.

Anne Bardsley

I collected mouse figurines, and this was my favorite one. I used it until I was thirteen!

When Dad came home, which was often late at night after we went to bed, he would always come in and kiss me goodnight. A simple kiss on the forehead and a "Goodnight, Dee Dee, I love you."

In 2015, my father passed away from cancer. I flew from Colorado to Georgia to meet my sister and see him in hospice. He had lived in my sister's guest room, which had become Daddy Dave's room.

When we arrived at the hospice to visit him, I was shocked when I saw him. Lying in that bed was a man who was thin and frail. He looked so much older than my dad. It was so hard to see my hero at the whim of this horrible disease. He slept almost the whole time we were there to visit. He did, however, reach up with both hands to indicate he wanted a hug, and I gladly leaned over him to give him a hug and a kiss on the forehead and tell him I loved him so very much.

I remember the night before he passed, whispering in his ear that it was okay to go. There was a "party" waiting for him in heaven, and I would be there soon. Not now, but one day in the future. "Jesus is waiting to welcome you, Dad. It's okay to go," I told him. At 4:00 a.m., we got the call that he had passed.

Three months later, I booked a trip back to Atlanta to visit my sister. We had become closer than ever. I remember flying in on September 20. I wanted to go out and have dinner and paint the town with my sister the next day. But I was too tired to go anywhere, so I settled for an early night turn-in. I was sleeping in the bed, in the very room where Dad had slept so many nights before his passing. At about 11:30 p.m., I closed my book and was going to reach over to turn the light off when I noticed the sheets pulling toward the side of the bed. I thought, *That's silly, I must be tired.* Then I felt it again and turned to look behind me. I saw the bed depress ever so slightly as if someone's knee was pressing on it. I was terrified.

I turned the bedside light on, then the overhead light as well. I looked under the bed to see if one of my sister's dogs was in the room. Maybe Dad's cat had found his way back home. Nothing. I finally crawled back into bed after turning the lights off and told myself I was silly.

Just as I was drifting off to sleep, I felt a gentle brush on my forehead. I remembered how Dad always came in and leaned over to kiss me goodnight. (Of course, I did brush my hand over my forehead, in case it was one of the notorious insects the South had to offer—it wasn't.) I have concluded that it was my father who made the impression on the bed that pulled the sheets, and the brush against my forehead, his gentle kiss.

He wasn't with us anymore, but he was with me that night, to say goodnight and goodbye. Now, when people talk about loved ones who have passed contacting those left behind, I have to say I know it happens. I watched the sheets move, the bed depress, and felt the brush of a gentle kiss that could not be explained any other way. It was truly the best "twenty-first night of September" anyone could have ever had! I got one last visit from my father.

I now live with my sister and occupy that same bedroom. We kept the beautifully carved sleigh bed he and she had found at an auction. It's now "my room," but still holds so much memory of our dad. I am not afraid of visits from the "other side" anymore. I only pray that in some ways he's still around. I welcome Angel Bumps. They are real, and they are precious!

DAWN REYNOLDS is hitting both sixty and the reset button on life as she's known it! She's amazed at what she can see when she stops running so fast to impress the world. She loves that her father's love is still with her—even though he's gone home ahead of her!

Cardinals, Chipmunks, and Angels

ANNE BARDSLEY

Our yard has been frequented by a bright red cardinal. He perches on a low branch where he can see through my kitchen window. His head twists from side to side as he chirps. He seems deep in conversation some mornings. If only I spoke the bird language!

Lately, my husband, Scott, has been remembering times with his grandmother, Nanny. Each story he shares about her makes me love her more. Now, there was a woman who spoke the bird language!

She'd leave her kitchen window open, and when she whistled, a cardinal would arrive and perch on her windowsill. If she worked in her garden, all she had to do was whistle and the cardinal would appear. When she moved to the front yard, he'd spread his wings to follow her.

Nanny had several visitors daily. One had feathers, and the other had a bushy tail. A chipmunk was equally enamored with her. She'd feed him nuts and seeds. She'd call him for lunch, and he'd arrive to sit at the table. If she was too slow getting his meal, he'd climb right up onto the table, waiting for his feast. She would chat with him while he nibbled his food. It could have been a commercial for Dr. Doolittle.

I knew that Nanny was very special to my husband, especially during his college years. He'd helped her at her apartment with chores. She, in turn, made him lunch and invited her nature friends into the kitchen to join them. He remembers these times vividly.

Speaking of enamored, Nanny loved her time with Scott. They'd sit on the couch and watch *Star Trek* together. The Vulcans with their pointy ears amused her. She wasn't a fan of the Romulans, with their enlarged heads. Her favorite was Spock. While she really had no idea what the show was about, she enjoyed the time with her oldest grandson. He still smiles when he tells that story.

Years ago, we visited Nanny in a nursing home. She propped herself up in bed and patted a spot for Scott to sit. She pulled his face in close, and with both hands holding his face, she said, "Oh, you're so pretty!" Then she smiled and her blue eyes sparkled. She died shortly after that visit.

I have a feeling that Nanny has been visiting us. The cardinal is a shining, brilliant shade of red. I talk to the bird: "Well good morning! Look at you!" I shower him with compliments and make small talk. Yes, I make small talk with a bird. I tell Nanny I'm taking good care of Scott, and I'm so happy she came to visit.

In our lifetime, Nanny's chipmunk is a squirrel at our house. He gets our attention by climbing our patio screen, directly in front of us. He clings to the screen and looks squarely at us. "Can you see me now?" This makes Scott crazy. He keeps a mint-scented squirt bottle near his chair.

It's supposed to deter squirrels, but no one gave that memo to our buddy.

I wish we'd had more time with Nanny. I loved her charming ways. We would have been best friends. After all, we have so much in common. How do I know this? Scott, the cardinal, and a squirrel told me so.

We love you, Nanny!

ANNE BARDSLEY is the author of this book. She has five adult kids and is a "Gigi" to five adorable little characters. And she does mean characters! She lives in St. Petersburg, Florida, with her sweet husband, Scott.

X-Ray Vision

KELLY MCKENZIE

My fiancé, John, was thrilled to be accepted into the highly competitive two-year medical imaging program at the age of thirty. Any hospital would be lucky to have him. His interactions with the worried and sick would be insightful because he truly understood the impact of simple things, such as calling someone by their first name, offering up a kind word, or even just a reassuring smile.

John had been in and out of hospital himself since he was thirteen. When a diagnosis of his symptoms proved ever elusive, his desperate mother sent his medical records to the Mayo Clinic. They confirmed what the perplexed Vancouver doctors could not. Her son was suffering from Crohn's disease.

I was twenty-seven and just weeks into my sales job in my mother's Asian antique shop when I first met Mrs. McKenzie. She had popped in looking for something colorful for her mantelpiece. We were chatting easily until she mentioned the unthinkable. "I was your mother's first customer in this location."

That revelation changed everything—this woman was guilty of buying the first thing I'd ever liked from Mom's inventory. It was a tiny antique hand-carved jade Chinese pig. I'd been religiously saving up for it when, suddenly, it was gone.

"I had to sell it, Kel. Mrs. McKenzie is giving the pig to her son, who's gravely ill in the hospital."

My mother's deep remorse meant little.

That was over a year ago. How was her son now? More importantly, did he appreciate the pig?

I would eventually get an update on both. It happened when I was seated next to a good-looking stranger at a brunch celebrating the completion of a 10K run, some four years later. He was my friend's new boyfriend; the rest of the folks around the table were fellow runners. As we chatted, I felt like we'd somehow met before; most of his stories were eerily familiar.

"What's your last name, John?"

"McKenzie. Why?"

"I thought so. Your mother shops at our store. You got my pig."

After a few heart-stopping seconds, I saw the recognition dawn. He broke out into a huge grin.

"The little hand-carved porker that Mom gave me? I love it."

Nothing gave me greater pleasure than when that couple broke up a few months later. I liked John. A lot.

We'd been married almost a year when John was hired after graduation to work at the local trauma hospital, a ten-minute commute away. His charisma and affability made him popular with patients, and his colleagues were soon treated to John's rather devilish sense of humor.

Our arguments never lasted long, thanks to John. After one memorable marital tiff, I flounced off to bed, but not before throwing open the bedroom window. It was a cold January night, and my husband preferred the room toasty warm; it would soon be frigid. Perfect. I awoke to find John climbing into bed wearing a toque, ski mitts, long underwear, and a heavy sweater. He didn't say a word. I was giggling before his head hit the pillow.

Our family grew. We welcomed a black Labrador puppy. Our daughter arrived next, and twenty months later, our son was born. John proudly schlepped all three into the hospital for show-and-tell regularly. Life was good, and I truly took his health for granted.

But then, just a few weeks shy of our daughter's third birthday, John's Crohn's suddenly flared up and he needed surgery. He batted away my concerns with an easy smile. "Don't worry, Kel. This, too, shall pass. I'll be out of this bed in no time."

But he wasn't. Complications arose and he ended up gravely ill in the Intensive Care Unit. My sister kindly took our kids and the dog, enabling me to spend hours at John's bedside or in the ICU waiting room. The one time I snuck out for lunch at a nearby restaurant, I was called to the phone. It was the hospital reporting that John had relapsed and required more surgery. Immediately.

Life limped along colorlessly for the next three weeks. And then it changed completely with a 5:00 a.m. phone call on January 29. The doctor was in tears, and I could barely make out his words. My heart ached for him. What a dreadful message to have to deliver to a mother of two young children. I had to help.

"He's gone, isn't he?"

The surgeon took a ragged breath and confirmed that John's weary body couldn't fight a moment longer. My thirty-eight-year-old husband had suffered a massive heart attack and passed away just moments ago.

My sister-in-law and I dashed to the hospital to discover that the staff had thoughtfully removed his bulky breathing tube, leaving my husband, while now paler than pale, looking as if he was peacefully sleeping. Maybe he was? I leaned in to kiss him. His cheek was colder than steel.

Time stopped.

We gradually became aware of the orderly fidgeting outside. He needed the room. I stumbled blindly out into the now coffin-like hallway only to bump into one of John's nurses. He swept me into his arms.

"I'm so very sorry, Kelly. We did everything we possibly could."

That revelation unleashed a fresh torrent of tears, and the crushing reality hit. My darlings' father was no longer alive. I was a widow with two young toddlers. How could I get through the day, let alone raise them all alone? I wasn't capable. But I had to be. How? I prayed for a sign, anything that would give me an inkling of hope.

Just then, an unusual rumbling noise, not unlike thunder off in the distance, pierced the tomb-like quiet. As it drew closer, I became aware of the sharp squeaks of rubber-soled shoes scrabbling for purchase on the freshly waxed floor.

"Look out!"

The three of us turned as one.

A large mobile X-ray machine came lumbering toward us, lurching from side to side with a frantic young nurse scrambling closely behind. It was startling. I'd spent every day of the past month here, and this was the first time I'd even noticed such an apparatus. What's more, there wasn't a slope in sight; this novelty was trundling along on a surface that was as flat as a deceased's cardiogram.

Just as I steeled myself to press up against the wall, the X-ray machine suddenly shunted and lurched to a halt at my feet. But it didn't shut down. Multiple lights flashed red in perfect tandem with a series of staccato beeps. It was thrumming with palpable energy.

The woefully out-of-breath wrangler began to babble.

"I'm so sorry. I was just prepping a patient for her humerus X-ray when this puppy suddenly came to life and took off!" Of course, it did.

I burst out into joyful laughter, to the shocked astonishment of everyone. Bless you, John, and message received. I *can* do this. With your help.

Twenty-five years later, John continues to send signs to his wife and their two children with unique and mischievous angel bumps.

FIND KELLY at https://kellylmckenzie.com.

BEN444

Janice Weiss

I'd like to share an Angel Bump that occurred seventeen years ago, a few months after my father died. I had just accepted a new job in Ohio and was commuting by plane back to my husband and kids in Connecticut every weekend for six months until they were able to make the move with me. It was an incredibly stressful time on many fronts, and I yearned for communication from my father, who claimed to be an atheist himself. For reasons that would take a long time to explain, I began to believe that anytime I saw the triple digit 444, it was a loving sign from my father.

Every day on my way back and forth from work, I would count the number of triple fours I saw on license plates. I seemed to see them everywhere—more than I should have by the odds of it alone—and it was somehow reassuring. As the summer rolled on, I was under significant pressure at work. One night after a very tough day at the office, I came back to my apartment and began bawling and calling out to my father. I was so scared and lonely. I wanted him to make it all better by giving me a sign. I yelled at him that he was driving me crazy.

Anne Bardsley

I told him I thought I was going out of my mind by seeing him in 444s. I was angry at him because if he was trying to communicate, why did he have to be so cryptic? Why not just flash the lights or turn on the radio, like a normal ghost? I thought I was going nuts, and I reminded him that when he was alive, we had often debated the after-life—he was a total, total skeptic—and so if he wanted me to believe it was him, he'd have to do a heck of a better job than license plates with 444!

After crying myself to sleep, I felt a little better in the morning. It was Friday, and I headed to the airport for my flight home. Normally I left via Cincinnati, but last minute, my assistant had booked me for the first time out of Columbus to save money. It was a two-hour car trip. My mind wandered as I drove. Just as I was getting close to the airport, suddenly a voice behind my right ear whispered my father's name: "Ben." It was a voice—not a thought, and not like anything I had ever experienced before. I would say it was a female voice, but I can't be sure. I just know it was audible, and it wasn't *my* voice. I immediately thought how unusual it was to hear the name Ben, since I probably hadn't heard anyone say his name since the funeral. And then I thought—wouldn't it be wonderful to see a license plate with BEN on it.

Within two seconds of that thought, to my amazement, for the first time I noticed a BEN license plate speed right past me. I was in awe—it felt like a call-out from the other side. But hold on—the story doesn't end there, by far. I knew while this was extraordinary to me, my well-meaning cynical friends and family would probably tell me that I saw the license plate first and then heard the "voice"—not the other way around—and that it was just my wishful mind playing tricks. I knew that wasn't the case, but I understood why they would think that.

I traveled back to Columbus that Sunday evening. The plane was very delayed, and we didn't arrive until close to midnight. Since it was a two-hour drive back to Cincinnati again, I decided to get a hotel room and leave at 6:00 a.m. instead. When I returned to the airport to pick up my car, I went to where I thought I had parked it. The lot was not very full, but in the exact space I was sure I had left my car, there was a car—but it was not mine! Instead, it was someone else's car, and the license plate on that car—believe it or not—was BEN444. I kid you not! I was stunned beyond words and called my husband, of course, and he was blown away as well. It was before camera phones, so I had no way of recording the event.

Anyway, I still couldn't find my car. I walked around, and to my amazement again, I saw two other BEN license plates within twenty feet of the first one. Triple BENs— extraordinarily cool if you ask me! (There was also a 111 license plate next to the original car, which has always been my signal from "God" or the "Universe.") I finally had to call security to ask them to help me find my car. It turns out that I had parked on the level the lot labeled "orange," and I had been searching on a level called "yellow," which if you had looked at the signs on the wall, you could have easily taken to be orange. Finally, I found my car parked exactly one floor below.

This is one of many unexplained experiences I have had over the years, and I have always thought of them as winks or hugs from beyond. They come when I need them most and provide just enough awakening and reassurance to let me know that things will be okay.

Anne Bardsley

As my father loved to quote: "Don't worry; be happy!"

JANET WEISS, a former New Yorker happily living in Cincinnati as a marketing executive. She is a grateful wife and the mom of two launched children. She's aging with wonder in her sixties.

The Lady in the Yellow Dress

MICHELLE CHERMAINE RAMOS

I never met my maternal grandmother—at least not while she was still alive. She passed away a few years before I was even born so I lost the opportunity to make many memories with her in life. But a single encounter with her after death cemented the existence of an afterlife in my young mind.

My earliest memory of having an otherworldly dream was around the age of six. In this dream, I traveled just outside the gates of heaven where a stranger came out to greet me. She was a smiling old lady in a yellow dress who introduced herself as my grandma.

I remember being taught as early as I could remember—well, as far back as any six-year-old could remember—to never trust strangers, let alone follow them. However, there was something about being with her in that environment and being around all the people or angels present that made me feel completely at ease, loved, and safe. I remember going on a tour and being overwhelmed with light and intense love and joy. We walked through a garden with flowers in more vibrant colors than I had ever seen in real life.

Anne Bardsley

After I woke up, I couldn't get the dream out of my head and felt an inexplicable burst of inspiration to record the whole experience the only way I knew how as a kid. Armed with coloring pencils and crayons, I drew my very first picture book on pieces of white paper folded and stapled with a scrap piece of cardboard as a cover.

With childlike innocence, I took my crudely constructed book to school and excitedly shared the story with the other kids in class and my teacher who, thankfully, did not think I was crazy. Or, at least, they were kind enough not to say so if they did. That afternoon at home, I took the book out of my backpack and showed it to my mom.

I narrated the dream that inspired the illustrations as if the whole experience were as real as the family vacation we took last summer. Although I had no idea what Grandma looked like when she was alive, as far as my six-year-old self was concerned, I truly believed that I met her in that dream and that the whole thing might as well have been real.

Then Mom confirmed something about it was real. When she saw the page with my drawing of Grandma in her yellow dress taking me for a walk in a heavenly garden, Mom's facial expression changed from curious to serious.

"Your grandma was buried in that yellow dress," Mom said. "She appeared to me too after she died."

Mom recounted those three days after grandma was buried; she saw her walking up the stairs of their home towards her. Unfortunately, for some mysterious reason, at that particular moment Mom forgot that Grandma was already dead.

Taking it in as just another normal scene at home, Mom simply walked into another part of the house, thinking nothing of it. Seconds later, as soon as the reality of who she had just seen hit her, Mom ran back to the staircase to look for Grandma, but she was already gone.

"She was walking up the stairs wearing the yellow dress she was buried in," Mom recalled.

To this day, Mom still doesn't understand how she got that temporary case of selective amnesia at the most inopportune moment. She figured maybe Grandma let it happen that way so that she wouldn't be alarmed at seeing her spirit. Then again, it's not like Mom would have been scared anyway. Grandma was not the first or only deceased member of our family who ever stopped by for a final good-bye—or in my case, a first hello.

Michelle is a poet, journalist, and intuitive artist in Toronto, Canada. She paints symbolic keepsakes of departed souls. Visit her at http://michellechermaine.com

The Night Midnite Came to Stay

PENNIE PYLANT

In October 2016, seven days before my daughter's thirteenth birthday, we discovered that she and her eleven-year-old brother's biological mother passed away. Mona died from an overdose. Her addiction brought so much pain into her children's lives. I wasn't sure how we'd ever recover as a family from this tragedy.

After we told the children the news, consoled them, and got them to sleep, I went outside to smoke. It was midnight, but I was restless and thinking of Mona.

I said, "Dang it, Mona, I can't believe you're gone," as I put out my cigarette.

Suddenly, I could feel her spirit, and she was sad, angry, and desperate to be heard.

I closed my eyes and said, "I want you to know that we'll take care of the kids. They are going to be just fine; no worries, okay?"

In my mind's eye, she showed me all the pain and trauma she had suffered in her life, along with huge regrets she had from past mistakes.

My heart ached for her. I said, "It's okay, you are free now. Nothing can hurt you ever again. You can go with love and know that I will try my best to be a good momma to our kiddos."

She showed me a huge heart.

I said, "Thank you, that means so much. Do me a favor, please, when you get to the other side, tell my people that I love and miss them and I'm doing the best I can."

And the heart multiplied into 2, 4, 8, 16, 32 hearts! I felt a warm embrace. I bowed my head, tears flowing free, and said,

"Thank you, Mona. Hey everybody! I love y'all and I will see y'all again one day."

I felt embrace after embrace, Granny Watson, DJ, Daddy, Grandmother Thomas, I could feel them all! I was overwhelmed with emotions, and I felt so blessed!

When I opened my eyes, a scruffy, black, kitten was sitting on my porch, just three feet away from me. I said, "Hi, Beautiful, I'm so glad you're here. She walked toward me and rubbed against my leg.

I gently stroked her fur. Her faded collar was too tight. It was embedded in her fur. She meowed, rubbed against my leg, jumped in my lap, and started purring.

She let me take the collar off her and I used my fingers to brush the briars and tangles from her soft fur. We sat like that for quite a while, as she kneaded my leg with her paws.

I felt at peace knowing Mona was watching over us. I wondered if this kitten was a sign, a gift from Mona. The kids would love this kitten.

I named her Midnite.

That's the night Midnite came to stay. She's our spiritual gift. Not only did Midnite need us, but we needed her. She went from a scrawny, unwanted kitten to a beautiful, loving part of our family. She reminds us every day that we have our very own guardian angel watching over our family.

PENNIE PYLANT lives on Lake Texoma in Texas with her partner, two teenage sons, two dogs and of course, Midnite. She's a grateful grandmother to a grandson and twin granddaughters.

Acknowledgments

I am deeply grateful for each author who shared their story in this volume. I'm honored to be present at such a sacred time in their lives.

I am beyond grateful to all those who support me, including writers in the Erma Bombeck Conference, my CHRP sisters at St John Vianney Church women's group, and especially my dear friend, Jeanie Fowler who allowed me to skip exercise class (guilt free) to finish this book.

A special thank you to my husband Scott. He has astounding patience with me and my computer skills. I am forever grateful that he doesn't run screaming into the hills. After forty-four years of marriage, I still love and cherish him.

I am grateful to God for entrusting me with a gift to help heal people's hearts. I often wonder if He remembers that I cried for three days after watching ET return home. I am not a fan of farewells. Yet, here I am.

I am very grateful to all the readers who have purchased *Angel Bumps, Hello from Heaven* and *Heartstrings From Heaven*. These books have wings of their own. They find people who need to know they are never alone. Oh! The stories I could tell you!

I am deeply grateful to Karen Fox Tarlton. She is the artist who painted the cover. You can feel her paintings in your heart. (She also painted the first *Angel Bumps, Hello From Heaven* and the upcoming *Angel Bumps, Pawprints From Heaven*.) Visit https://www.karensfinearts.com.

If you enjoyed this book, please leave a review on Amazon/Goodreads. Reviews matter!

Read Book One in the Angel Bumps Series:

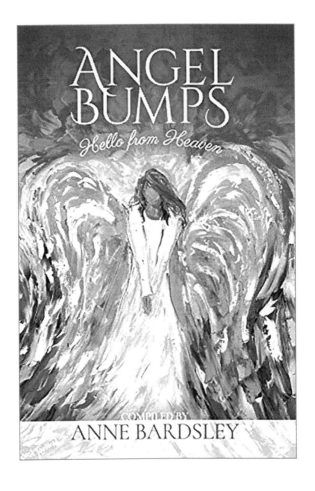

Follow my blog: www.annebardsley.com

Join the Angel Bumps group page on FB

Contact me at myangelbumps@gmail.com

Anne Bardsley is the author of *How I Earned My Wrinkles, Angel Bumps: Hello from Heaven,* and *Heartstrings from Heaven: Book Two in the Angel Bumps Series.* Her writing has appeared in *Chicken Soup for the Soul, Guidepost Magazine, The Grand,* the website for Erma Bombeck, and several other publications. She's a Gigi to five beautiful and comical grandchildren. She's married to the love of her life, Scott, and lives in St Pete, Florida.